AF228435

"*Push, Then Breathe* is a book about the painful emergence of a woman who overcomes personal trauma to become a healer and a model of inspiration to others. Her journey provides a roadmap to all who suffer and offers a way out through a deep commitment to an inspirational vision."

—Roger Saillant, PhD, author of *The Power of Being Seen*, entrepreneur, executive leader

"*Push, Then Breathe* challenges and inspires readers with its unflinching honesty and heartfelt grace. Dr. Kiprono has written a story that describes her own captivating journey and beautifully addresses critical issues many people face each day. It is a must-read for anyone who is dealing with trauma or for those who are looking for a book to make them cheer."

—Brian Lawrence, PhD, MEd, MA, Keystone School, San Antonio, TX

PUSH, THEN BREATHE

PUSH, THEN BREATHE

TRAUMA, TRIUMPH, AND THE
MAKING OF AN **AMERICAN** DOCTOR

DR. LUISSA KIPRONO, MBS, MBA

GREENLEAF
BOOK GROUP PRESS

This book is a memoir reflecting the author's present recollections of experiences over time. Its story and its words are the author's alone. Some details and characteristics may be changed, some events may be compressed, and some dialogue may be recreated. Some names and identifying characteristics of persons referenced in this book, as well as identifying places, have been changed to protect the privacy of the individuals and their families.

Published by Greenleaf Book Group Press
Austin, Texas
www.gbgpress.com

Distributed by Greenleaf Book Group

For ordering information or special discounts for bulk purchases, please contact Greenleaf Book Group at PO Box 91869, Austin, TX 78709, 512.891.6100.

Design and composition by Greenleaf Book Group
Cover design by Greenleaf Book Group
Cover Images by Sylverarts Vectors from Shutterstock.com and Kodochigov from istockphoto.com

Publisher's Cataloging-in-Publication data is available.

Print ISBN: 979-8-88645-150-4

eBook ISBN: 979-8-88645-151-1

To offset the number of trees consumed in the printing of our books, Greenleaf donates a portion of the proceeds from each printing to the Arbor Day Foundation. Greenleaf Book Group has replaced over 50,000 trees since 2007.

Printed in the United States of America on acid-free paper

23 24 25 26 27 28 29 30   10 9 8 7 6 5 4 3 2 1

First Edition

To Mami, my light.
To Jordan and Brendan, my life.
To Charles, "bold is best."

**To all the women of the world: may my journey
serve as a lighthouse for your brave heart,
your clear mind, your true soul.**

CONTENTS

FOREWORD

Life for everyone is full of victories and challenges. We are all the sum of our accrued experiences.

But many people have experienced amazing successes over what seem to be insurmountable challenges. When these people share their victories over what seem to be overwhelming obstacles, we all gain hope and personal insight into our own life tapestries. Within this book, Dr. Luissa Kiprono defines personal strength, understanding, and victory over significant challenges! This book is her story, her tapestry, and her victory.

I was always aware that Dr. Kiprono was special. Her devotion to the greater good, her single-minded commitment to personal and patient-care excellence, and an inner strength related to situational self-awareness were and are easy to spot in Luissa. However, I never knew her story until I read her manuscript. I now have the privilege of knowing much more about her and of the tapestry that makes her who she is.

Dr. Kiprono grew up outside the United States during a time of great social upheaval. Early in her life, Luissa and her family survived the unraveling social myth of Eastern European Communism. Her story of those times, and how she prospered and excelled within her country's chaotic, arbitrary, and oppressive society is an inspiring read in and of itself. Her search for truth and for what was right and good prevailed in a system designed to stifle anything but survival. However, it is the second part of the story that demonstrates her resilience and strength. Without telling her whole story in this foreword, Luissa overcame isolation, betrayal, and abuse and achieved a degree of success in a way that is unparalleled. Not only did she prevail, she thrived!

Personal stories are often judged by their results. And as I noted, her results were and are phenomenal. However, I believe the lesson that she most powerfully illustrates is *how* she navigated through the challenges she faced. Not giving up, always looking for the good and positive in situations and circumstances, and the seeking of both justice and mercy in her journey are priceless takeaways for the reader. Those of us who are ourselves survivors of violence and brutality receive the gift of understanding resilience. We also learn to forgive and protect ourselves as we forgive others. An underlying theme of self-care and awareness echoes within her words. So, while the story is about overcoming external forces, it is the internal victory Luissa achieved that is the true triumph.

I believe readers will come to understand the power of purpose and the victory that comes from perseverance and believing in oneself. And, as one looks deeper, readers will also see the true beauty and grace of her story: turning a story of evil and hate into one of love.

James W. Van Hook, MD
Sheely Professor and Chair
Department of Obstetrics and Gynecology
University of Toledo College of Medicine
and Life Sciences, Toledo, Ohio

SECTION I

FIRST LIFE IN ROMANIA (BIRTH)

"We delight in the beauty of the butterfly, but rarely admit the changes it has gone through to achieve that beauty."
—Maya Angelou

1

EARLY GRACE

Suzette purred and slid her soft body across my shins as I sat in the shade of the oak tree, a book splayed open on my belly and my eyes closed. I breathed deeply. In, out. In, out.

The late-afternoon air was beginning to cool. I sat up, tugged my sweater against my body, and tucked my knees tight against my chest, my spine curved against the hard trunk of my favorite tree. Suzette gave me a cool look as she meandered away from me, finding her favorite gravestone and rubbing her body forcefully against the slab. I watched her fluid movements and heard her purr louder as she rubbed against the rough edge.

I absently lifted a hand to my newly shaven head, rubbing the spiky hairs under my palm. I breathed again, this time sharply, and my stomach convulsed, a sick feeling washing over me as I tried to push reality from my mind. This graveyard was my brief daily escape, my time to be free, with my cat and surrounded by lives and stories not my own.

My gaze drifted across the railroad tracks that ran along the cemetery, to the apartment where I lived with my father. My stomach clenched and I quickly looked away. Turning back toward the headstones, my thoughts drifted to Romania, where my mom and extended family still lived, where I would give anything to be, surrounded by the purity and ease of their love. Except I couldn't return to them yet. I didn't see how I could until I made things right. I was here, in America, the land of the free, a place of promised possibilities. A country of hope and potential. But America represented anything but freedom to me. It was a place where I was imprisoned, where my life had broken into pieces, where I'd come undone. It was 1989. I was 21, and all I could do was keep going forward, day by day, clinging wildly to my dream of someday becoming a doctor.

A doctor. It was all I had wanted since fifth grade. Becoming a physician was the noblest career I could imagine. The ability to heal others, to save them . . . it was my calling. Being called "doctor" for the first time would be a momentous experience. I sighed deeply at the thought: Doctor Vrâncuţa. The suffering, the sacrifice, the pain, the tears, the fear—I could put it all behind me. I could leave my father behind, along with this godforsaken apartment and the memories. I could lock up my years with him deep within my mind, never to be opened again.

Suzette was curled up next to me now, her warm spine pressing against my hip. Leaning my head back on the wide trunk, I closed my eyes and took another deep breath. This was my only space to recharge, to find myself, to anchor to the Luissa I'd been before I came to America, the girl I knew was still inside of me. To find the strength to go on another day.

Just then, a blip of a memory struck me: my mom standing above me, her face with loving blue eyes and a warm smile surrounded by blond, wavy hair. Her small hands holding my dimply cheeks, her palms warm on my face.

Picturing my mom caused a feeling of strength to wash over me. The sun peeked out from behind a cloud, flooding my face with light. I placed my palms on the grass, feeling their stringy-sharp blades, running my fingers along their tips. Sliding my sandals off, I laid my bare soles on the grass, feeling its cool, fresh brush under my feet. Yes, to be connected, grounded, steady, even if only for a moment. Peace. I basked in it.

The thought came quickly: *I must get back.*

I clicked my tongue at Suzette and reached out my fingers to pet her head gently. She looked up to me, and I stood. After stretching, she stood too, waiting next to me as I gathered my book under my arm and patted my shoulder. Then she jumped up, scaling the height of my body to land squarely on my left shoulder, her paws massaging my tense shoulders as she balanced. I petted her head and she nuzzled my cheek. Her friendship was my armor. I pulled her into my arms, and we made our way back to hell.

—

I was born in Brăila, a port city on the Danube River in eastern Romania, on May 18, 1968, the same day as the late Pope John Paul II, who was born forty-eight years earlier. But while the Pope's young life was marked by loss—the death of his mother and brother in childhood; later fleeing his country; the death of his father—my childhood was cocooned in family. Protected. I was treated like a family treasure, a child of hope and possibility. Future doctor, golden child, belle of the ball. My curly blond hair bounced when I laughed, and my mom's pride beamed on me when I entered a room.

My parents' relationship began with long glances that turned into conversation, and eventually a long-distance relationship that lasted through three years of dating and one of a short marriage. My father was a ticket collector on a train, my mom a passenger traveling cross-country from the eastern port of Brăila to the western city of Timișoara with my grandparents. Surely my mother's appearance caught his attention: blond hair set against blue eyes and a petite five-foot frame. It was 1964 and my mother, just eighteen years old at the time, said a shy "yes" when the young ticket collector asked for her number after a short conversation.

Years later, Bunica, my grandmother, would rant: "Damn it, I wish he had lost that number."

Their long-distance relationship began shortly after that trip. They talked on the phone several times a week. He would visit her in Brăila; she would travel the fourteen hours by train to Timișoara to see him. But even so, they never truly dated, not with the depth that would have enabled them to know each other in a real way.

When they married three years after that fateful train ride, in August 1967, nobody from his family attended the ceremony. They later had a small celebration in his birthplace, Globu Craiovei, then moved to Timişoara to start their life together. My mother was a virgin on their wedding night and became pregnant shortly after they were married.

The marriage lasted only eight months.

As my mom's stomach grew, so did her unease with her new situation in Timişoara. When she moved across Romania to be with her husband, she left her family behind for the dream of building a new one and took a job as a teller at a bank. Like any bride, she had been hopeful. Ready to embrace married life and soon, motherhood. I imagine her during those years: learning to cook, eagerly preparing a nursery, trying hard to be a good wife.

But life with her new husband wasn't anything like the bright, happy ideal she'd envisioned. By the third month of marriage, my parents were living apart, with my father at the college dorms and my mom living in cramped quarters with her aunt Katerina—my grandfather's sister—and her family of seven. My father claimed that the separate living quarters were necessary because of the distance between his school and her work. Rather than starting a new life together, they were growing apart, and she sensed there was more going on at the dorms than he let on. She had heard one whispered hallway conversation and could detect his growing detachment. And she was right; my father was living a double life. One of a young, single college boy; the other of a married man who would be thirty-one years old by the time he graduated.

As he lived the life of a bachelor, she was living with her aunt in a small house full of people, sleeping on a cot in the hallway. When he did visit, he wouldn't say a word to her family. He would come, visit with my mom, and then leave. No "how are you doing" or "thank you for taking in my pregnant wife." Not even a hello or goodbye.

This behavior insulted and baffled her family. But my mom knew the reason behind his actions. My father believed he was too important to interact with anyone below his station. Of course, his station wasn't high: He was a college student without two *lei* to rub together. He didn't come from money, he didn't have an impressive job, and he wasn't highly revered at his college.

But still, he considered those less educated—her family, and even most members of his own peasant family—beneath him. The one exception he made was for his mother, whom he admired for her Swedish heritage.

One day, when she was nearly eight months pregnant with me, my mother looked around at her life and knew she couldn't raise her child there, in her aunt's stuffed home, with her husband visiting infrequently between school and whatever else he was doing. She decided to leave for Brăila and bring me up with her parents and her sister's family.

She tried to explain her point of view to my father. But rather than try to save their marriage, he told her that if she left, she could never come back. Their marriage, which was already broken, was over.

It wasn't long before she was back in Brăila, in my grandparents' home. Just like at her aunt's, their tiny space was bursting with people: my grandparents, my aunt and uncle, and then my mom. But as crowded as it was, she was surrounded by love. They slept three in one small bed: my mom, Bunica, and Aunt Gaby, whom I called Tutti. Uncle Alex, whom I called Sandu, slept on a couch, and Bunicu—my grandpa—in another small bed. I sometimes imagine my mom sleeping in a corner of the bed at night, a quilt pulled over her small frame, the walls lined with family photos, street light floating in from the window, cradling her belly. I think of her strength, facing the shame of a broken marriage in 1968 in Romania. Did she suffer? Was she scared? She must have felt afraid, even though she was surrounded by the safety of family.

Years later, Bunica told me, "Your mom never complained, was never resentful of the situation she found herself in. Quite the contrary. She was hopeful and happy to carry you in her belly, a testament of her love; all those feelings she had before for your father naturally transferred to you, like a renewed river, never to run dry or stagnant. You are the only thing she lives for, and she is content with it. Besides you, nothing else matters to her."

And so I was born that May of 1968, to a house full of people and love. My mom named me Luissa Daniela Vrâncuța, giving me the name of a man who would be absent in my life for more than nineteen years. Of course, my mother didn't know at the time what was ahead of us, only that she would do everything in her power to protect her daughter. Looking at my tiny face, she knew. Nothing, and nobody, would harm her baby. She would do anything to give me everything.

—

My father came to visit me two weeks after I was born, one of three times he would venture across the country from Timișoara to see me during childhood. As my mother would tell me years later, it was a chilly spring day, biting and crisp. In Romania, we have four distinct seasons, and the weather stays a true spring until June; we don't step lightly into seasons like other parts of the world do. So even in May it was cold enough to need a coat outside. Anytime they left the house with me—to visit a doctor or just get some fresh air—they cocooned me in blankets and made sure my bonnet was firmly on my head, covering my mop of hair.

My father's visit was met with tension, especially from my grandfather, who blamed my father for ruining my mom's life. Not wanting to stay in the apartment with the family, my father decided to take me outside to get some fresh air. As he lifted the bassinet I was sleeping in, dressed only in my onesie, my grandmother stopped him.

"It's cold," she said, motioning toward the light clothing I wore to sleep inside the heated home. "She needs something to keep warm."

My father brushed off her concern. "She's going to get tough."

He slid out the door without even grabbing a blanket as my grandmother stared worriedly after him.

When my father came back twenty minutes later, my skin was red and my extremities were cold. My mom rushed to cover my body, my fingers tiny icicles, and my grandmother shook her head in worry. My father left shortly afterward. He had a train to catch, back to Timișoara.

Within hours, I developed a fever. I began coughing, and my mother saw the space between my ribs suck in deeply as I grunted for oxygen.

"We need to take her to the hospital," my grandmother said. "Now."

At this, my family sprang to action. My mom put on her overcoat and scooped me into her arms as my grandmother helped her wrap me in swaddling clothes and cover me with a thick blanket; we did not have a car, so they walked to the hospital. My mom held me tightly as she rushed through the hospital to the emergency department, where I was immediately admitted. A quick glance and listen by the elderly physician, Dr. Buhu, convinced him that I needed to be rushed to the intensive care unit and administered oxygen.

What must it have been like for my mom, hovering over my limp body, wondering if her newborn baby girl would return home?

Later that evening, the nurse touched my mom's arm. "I think it's time to baptize her. I don't think she is going to make it."

As a nun sprinkled water on my forehead and my mother choked back sobs, I gasped for breath in the plastic hospital bassinet. My mother prayed for God to save me.

It would take several days for my lungs to regain their strength and for the doctor to decide I was well enough to go home. In my mom's retelling, the fact that I was healthy enough to leave the hospital did not ease her mind entirely. Instead, after she took me home and placed me in my bed to sleep, she studied my breathing intently all night, watching for signs of distress. Over the next weeks, Dr. Buhu visited regularly to check on me, each time assuring my mom that I was improving. But his positive reports did not ease her concern; her watchful eyes hovered closely over me each day and night.

Years later, my mom would share that something broke inside her then, but something grew in her too. Because you can't watch your child come close to death and not be changed. Already my greatest protector, my mother anchored herself in the work of motherhood. The goal was to raise me to be kind, cultured, disciplined, and fearless. Surrounded by family. Safe and healthy. Never feeling lack of any sort.

My father was wrong. I didn't need to get tough. I already was. And I had the toughest woman to raise me, too.

—

I was lucky I fell ill when I did. In the early 1960s in Romania, the health care system was on par with most Western European medical systems. But starting in the late 1960s, the health of Romanian citizens began to decline, and around 1970, mortality rates started worsening. The reason is simple: Romania was beginning to slip slowly and forcefully into poverty and social upheaval because of communism.

In 1968, the year I was born, communism was livable. The communist party had taken power more than two decades earlier, claiming totalitarian control of the country. The government claimed ownership of private businesses and limited the ability of churches to freely function, because religious freedom was seen as a threat to government control. Farming became centralized, with students from middle and high school eventually doing mandated rotations in fields. At the same time, Romanian art, culture, and intellectual pursuits were curated and weaponized for communism, with artists and intellectuals creating works that supported the regime. The four liberties as we once knew them—freedom of speech, gathering, worship, and press—were heavily monitored and censored. Fear of repercussions set the rule. The government aimed to ban all Western influence and keep the public's focus on Romanian scholars and artists.

By 1960, however, some of these intense efforts to squelch individualism and control the population had calmed. Access to food and other goods became more accessible, health care improved, artists began creating works that had previously been banned, and life in general felt somewhat normal, especially for those who had just endured more than a decade of tense communist control. When Nicolae Ceaușescu came into power three years before my birth, he didn't seem like a threat to the relative peace and freedom Romanian citizens felt, even under the thumb of the government.

If you minded your business and did what you needed to do, the Securitate—the secret, state-run police agency that monitored citizens and punished those who broke laws or went against the government—wouldn't bother you. My family didn't ruffle feathers, so our life was relatively normal. But the mark of communism still pulsed through my family's everyday life.

For instance, the fact that they didn't own anything. Not my grandfather's butcher shop, which he ran like a business owner, getting up at four o'clock in the morning to open the front doors each day, hiring and firing employees, running the daily operations, and worrying over the finances. Not our apartment, which they paid for through their heavily taxed labor and property fees. Not their voices, because they had to be careful what they said and who they said it to. Not their choice of books or radio: It was prohibited to read or listen to anything that was perceived as anti-Marxist, anti-Leninist doctrine. And not their daily schedules, because when the government held rallies, attendance was mandatory.

Yet while the subtle tension of communism bled through our entire country, things were still manageable. My family had a comfortable place to live, even if it was crammed with people; we had plenty of the basic food staples, including meat, eggs, cheese, and seasonal vegetables; my mom could afford to buy me clothes and the basics a baby required. They could even save enough extra money to pay for the once or twice per year road trips and occasional movie tickets. My family wasn't rich, but we had enough. And while I was too young to understand what was going on around me, surely I felt the love and security of a family that also felt connected and safe.

Like so much else in my young life, my country's relative stability wouldn't last. Outside the cocoon of my family home, Romania was in transition. It wouldn't be long before my childhood would shift drastically. Yet through all the coming upheaval, my family and that love would remain steady, an unbroken drumbeat sounding throughout my entire life.

I can't help but reflect now, half a century later, on how lucky I was back then. Fortunate, of course, not to die, but also lucky to be born into the family I was. Because later I would experience trauma that could break a person—that could have led to addiction, difficulty forming relationships, a tendency toward self-sabotage. But there, in that family, in the safety of the people who cherished me, even within a system as fraught with fear and danger as communism, I had security and love.

Not all children are so fortunate. Not all babies feel fully protected, with not one or two but *five* adults cooing over a bassinet, fretting over my tears, and ensuring all my needs were met. Not all kids grow up feeling cared for and strong, as though they can do anything—become anything. But even without a father, and even with what was to come, I was lucky.

My early childhood years anchored me for the trials and tribulations that would follow. That early grace would hold me up in the hardest times. And eventually, it would save me.

2

SUFFERING AND LOVE

I lay on my back, listening to the breathing of my kindergarten classmates napping around me. Fidgeting, I made a tent with my fingers, blowing through my lips to make quiet puff sounds, itching my leg. The creak of the door and the growing sliver of light stopped me. As I closed my eyes and flattened my hands on my stomach, I willed my body to hold still until I heard the soft click of the door being shut again.

Was my teacher gone? Was it safe to get up now?

But before I sat up, I heard the soft sound of footsteps. I counted to myself slowly to stay focused on being quiet and calm. *Unu, doi, trei . . .*

The steps padded closer to me as I tried to stay still.

Patru, cinci, șase. The footsteps stopped and I felt a presence above me. I wanted so much to scratch my arm and shift in my bed, but I also wanted to look asleep, so I kept silently counting.

Șapte, opt, nouă. Finally, my teacher's steps began again. I heard the door shut and the sound of her walking away. I knew she wouldn't be back for at least another half an hour.

Zece. Now.

I slowly turned and propped myself onto my elbows, looking around the dim room at the unmoving shapes of my friends napping peacefully in our kindergarten classroom. How did they fall asleep? I had never been able to fall asleep at school. There was so much to think about!

Quietly, I stood, pulling my blanket up to my pillow to make it look like I was still there. My gaze drifted to my doll, Angela Similea, named after a beautiful Romanian pop star. Angela sat high on a shelf I couldn't reach, thanks to Ms. Roman, our mean teacher.

The other kids called Ms. Roman an old maid. I just knew she could be scary. Her face frightened us: eyes squinting from behind reading glasses, eyebrows raised, creased forehead in a stern expression. When she came in the room, we'd all stop laughing and playing and freeze. We didn't want to be on Ms. Roman's bad side.

But even though I was scared of her, I wasn't going to let that stop me.

I walked silently across the floor, between my friends sleeping on small, thin cots. When I reached the door, I held my breath and pushed it open.

Ms. Roman is going to be so mad at me, I thought—as I walked out and closed the door behind me—when she found me gone . . . again.

But I didn't care if she would be mad. All I cared about was finding my mom. I hated going to school and having to leave her each day. And it was mean to take my doll. So fine, I would be on my way.

Once outside, I blinked in the bright sunlight.

Then I saw the gate. I hoped it wasn't locked.

I ran across the cobblestone courtyard and yanked on the big iron handle of the metal gate. It creaked open and I slid through.

Then I ran.

Now I just needed to find my way home.

So I wandered, looking at buildings and people and plants and bugs. I crossed busy streets using the crosswalk like my mom had taught me and peered into shops. Walking, looking, exploring—that's what I wanted to do, and find home, not take a nap.

I was looking at a dress in the window display of a clothing shop when I heard car doors open and shut behind me. I turned to see a police car and two policemen.

"Luissa," the shorter one said, "your mother is worried about you."

"You've gotta stop leaving like this," the tall one added.

I dropped my eyes and smoothed down my blue-checkered uniform, getting it dirty. My hands were covered in dirt from one of my bug explorations. Finally, I looked at them.

"She took my doll," I finally said. "My teacher."

The cops looked at each other. The short one walked toward me and squatted down to meet my eyes.

"You can't keep leaving school," he said. "You could have been hurt."

"Is my mom mad?" I asked.

"Let's get you home," he said. He stood and then opened the back door to the car.

I got in. I knew my mother wouldn't raise her voice because she didn't do that. But she'd give me that disappointed look that made me feel sad. I just wanted to make her happy. Some days it was too hard to stay at school, though, and I had to escape.

The car began to move and I watched the city go by as the police officers drove me home.

—

I was right, my mother didn't yell at me that day. Instead, she ripped me open with a long, silent gaze. I hung my head in shame at the guilt of disappointing her. My mother was my world, after all, and me, hers. She existed to make me feel safe and loved. I also knew she worried over me—and my now-thrice escapade through Brăila didn't calm her concerns.

It also didn't help that I was a sickly child. I was in and out of doctors' offices with chronic tonsillitis and sinusitis. The recurring sickness, combined with the steady stream of antibiotics I was prescribed, knocked my appetite out completely. I barely ate, refusing even the finest steaks and cuts of meat my grandfather brought home from the butcher shop just for me. Each time we saw Dr. Oliva, my pediatrician, Mom insisted that I needed my tonsils out, but the doctor assured her I would be fine. When I became immune to ampicillin antibiotics and had to move to Augmentin, she assured my mom again: "*Luissa va fi bine.*" Luissa will be fine.

Because of ongoing nausea, my diet consisted of four basic foods: eggs, tomatoes, bread, and *mititei*, ground cow's neck rolled into small sausages, mixed with garlic and spices like coriander and thyme, and grilled. My mom would cut the mititei into little discs—*soldăței*, little soldiers—and serve them with bread and dipping sauces: mustard or *mujdei de usturoi*, garlic sauce. I'd eat the meat with toothpicks, one piece at a time, tiptoeing past my nausea as I ate. These four foods were enough to keep me from becoming malnourished.

That, and *șatou de ou*, egg hot ice cream. Since cold ice cream would highly irritate my tonsils, my mother would heat up egg yolks, slowly pour in hot milk, and add sugar and sometimes cocoa. I always drank it slowly, savoring the rich taste as the warm, smooth liquid soothed my throat.

I was a well-behaved child at home, but my illness and eating distressed my mother, grandparents, Aunt Tutti, and Uncle Sandu. Before I started attending school, it was easy to get away with not eating because I was with Mama Oca, my nanny. Because I was so fussy and would only eat a few select items, my mother provided all three meals and, as part of her pay, would often send Mama Oca home with food.

Each day after my mother arrived home from work and hugged and kissed me hello, she'd ask Mama Oca, "How is Luissa doing?" The question held a clear subtext: Did Luissa eat today? To which my nanny would reply, "*Da, da! A mâncat.*" Yes, yes! She's eating. And then she'd tell my mom about the oranges I ate. She always mentioned oranges.

I hated oranges. The citrus stung my throat and the flavor unbearably punched my palate, sending shocks up to my sinuses. No, oranges were off the table, literally and figuratively.

The truth was, I was hardly eating. Mama Oca cared about me, and I know she wasn't intentionally protecting my self-starvation. If it wasn't eggs, tomato, bread, or mititei . . . well, I wasn't eating it. And even then, I usually refused my meals.

Over time, my lack of eating became more and more noticeable, even with Mama Oca's assurance that I was eating breakfast and lunch. Each time I would refuse my grandfather's best cuts of meat at dinner, he'd sigh, his loving eyes enveloping me as if trying to protect me, and say with that gentle voice he always used just for me, "*Obleţul lui Bunicu mic, de ce nu mănînci?*" Grandpa's little *oblét*, why won't you eat?

An oblét is a small, thin fish with a shimmering body and thin back of the head. He'd often rub my neck, telling me I had the neck of an oblét and needed to eat. I was a growing girl, after all. But no amount of encouragement or doting could heal the nausea that plagued me from wake to sleep. On top of that, the doctor noticed a heart murmur at my last appointment, and told my mother I was developing myocarditis, an inflammation of the heart muscle, likely from the numerous bouts of tonsillitis. At the age of seven, I weighed just seventeen kilos, about thirty-seven pounds, which was well below average for my height. My poor mother worried over me, taking me back to the doctor again and again, insisting I was seriously unwell and something more needed to be done.

It was around this time that we started taking trips to the ocean on the advice of our doctor, who said the salty sea air would help my upper respiratory ailments. Brăila is on the plains, so the air is more stagnant than it is by the ocean. Combined with the inevitable pollution of city life, the theory was that my environment was contributing to my sickness. Mom had two weeks' vacation a year, so our entire family began taking trips to the beach. Since we could not afford a car, all our trips were by train. We spent time in the seaside towns of Constanţa or Mamaia, or in the mountainous towns of Braşov or Predeal, where the clean mountain air and negative ions from the sea helped my breathing. The beach towns were next to each other, dotting the coast of Romania, so we'd often take the shuttle bus from place to place, exploring the towns and coastlines.

At the beach, I would build castles in the fine sand and play in the shallow water my grandmother insisted was too cold for swimming, or I'd stroll with Mom and collect seashells, studying their beauty in detail as I decided which ones to keep. Sometimes I would run up and down the vast expanse of sand, my mother looking after me as she lay on a towel next to my aunt, a broad smile on her face as she watched to make sure I didn't wander too far. The sea made me almost well, and that was motivation enough for my family to save year-round to afford these trips.

Taking these yearly trips to the Black Sea, along with growing up near the Danube River, was a powerful influence on me. Being near the water helped me find peace and connect with my inner self. I only realized how much so later in life, when I lived in areas here in America far from the water and the lack of access to it made me feel incomplete. I would long for its presence. Even in childhood, before I knew how much I needed the water, I knew I loved these trips.

Back at home in Brăila, family life continued to revolve around me. When I went to first grade, Bunica retired from her retail job at a small bread shop at the *piaţă*, the market, so she could stay home with me. Bunicu was firm in his conviction that his granddaughter would have someone at home after school. My mom worked hard as an economist for the city of Brăila, putting her knack for numbers to use during the day to provide for us. When she wasn't working, her attention was 100 percent on me. My Aunt Tutti, who had recently graduated college with a degree in Slavic languages, worked as a Russian teacher and spent her spare time doting on me like her own daughter. My Uncle Sandu, who had finished veterinary school, worked up through the ranks to become the regional director of the main sector of livestock and cereals aggregate in the Great Brăila Island; like his wife, he treated me like his own. Bunicu got up each day at four o'clock to open his shop, arriving home each evening with meats for me, his eyes lighting up when he saw his little love, his Luissa, with the golden curls and big smile just for him.

Sometimes I would visit Bunicu at work. His butcher shop was small and long, almost like a corridor. Meat hung from the ceiling, and to the right was a glass counter displaying expertly cut pieces of meat. In the back of the shop were two big blocks of wood made from tree trunks the size of a four-person family table, where he and his two helpers would cut meat. In the very back were the walk-in refrigerator where animal carcasses were neatly hanging from hooks, a tiny bathroom, and a breakroom where I would often sit, clutching my doll and waiting for him to take a break.

As I waited, I would peer at the room around me, taking in the sights and sounds. I was a curious and inquisitive child with an insatiable desire to learn new things. When my bunicu finally joined me, I would ask a lot of "why" questions until my little mind was satisfied with the answers, then I would mull over them while I waited for him again. So much to learn and think about—fascinating!

Entering the shop was like transporting to Bunicu's world: the earthy-sweet smell of raw meat that always clung to my grandfather's clothes and skin after a long day of work; the exchanges with customers as he handed over paper-wrapped packets of steaks, hamburger meat, and ribs; the smile that swept his face when he saw the door push open and had to peer over the counter to see his golden granddaughter staring up at him and asking, "Can I help?" If I came to visit late enough in the day, I'd get to watch him clean the blood and bones from the blocks and apply a thick coat of rock salt on top of them, smoothing the rough grains over the surfaces until they were entirely covered. The salt inhibited bacterial growth, and in the morning, he'd wash the block down with hot water and use it again for that day's cutting.

Thanks to my family, I had a normal, happy upbringing. They did everything they could to spare me the pain of the void left by my father.

My mother raised me with patience, reason, fairness, and love. She didn't believe in abusive language or punishments, but instead, taught me through stories, example, and some occasional tough love. She praised my strengths and would even occasionally buy me small gifts like a new book or my favorite pastry, items that may be taken for granted in a land of abundance but are quite special in countries like Romania. These gifts made me feel cared for.

Along with love and attention, my mother's strategy included providing me with a strong cultural education. At five, she enrolled me in gymnastics and ballet, which were always taught together in Romania. We weren't well off, but we had enough to live comfortably, take our annual holiday, and for my mom to pay for my lessons. I felt enveloped in safety and love.

Still, sometimes when we'd walk through the city or go to Central Park or take a trip to the store, I'd see a girl my age with her father, holding his hand without even realizing her immense fortune. I'd eye families—whole, complete families with a mother and father and one or more children—sitting together on blankets in the grass or on a park bench or buying lettuce at the store or standing in line at the cinema. I wasn't wanting for love, but I knew some kids had something I didn't. They had a father.

I would ponder this for a moment, and then, with the mind of a child, the thought would be hushed away.

—

On the other side of the country, my father was in Timișoara. He had remarried and moved on, having only visited me once more when I was about eighteen months old. He was covertly working against the communist party with a small group of his colleagues from college, reading volumes of books about capitalism and listening to banned radio stations from a large receiver in his home. He took part in an anti-communist revolution in Timișoara, of which he claimed to be the leader.

My father had always been on the outside, not quite fitting into the boxes set for society. Growing up in a village located in the mountainous land of Globu Craiovei, in the southwestern region of Romania, there was a clear path laid out for him: become a farmer and help the family. As the youngest of five children, he looked up to his two brothers and two sisters, but never could quite catch up with them in terms of perceived success and parental affection. Even as a child, he was a nonconformist, swept up in academics and wanting to pursue further education. As a teen, he became an athlete. He crafted his own wooden skis and would spend hours hiking up a mountain near his family's cottage home and gliding down, then hiking back up again, over and over. He took up Tae Kwon Do, drawing stares from people in his village as he did calisthenics outdoors. As a young adult, he developed the habit of regularly jumping in the Belareca tributary of the Cerna River in the dead of winter to strengthen his immune system. The villagers, and even his immediate family, thought he was crazy. His family members were devout Baptists, something he never seemed to embrace, judging by the way he lived his adult life: smoking, drinking, and chasing women.

Despite his interests and ambitions, he was still expected to do his part to help the family farm. So on days when he'd watch the animals while they were grazing, he would bring a book and read or study under a tree. In the evenings, after his work in a uranium mine, he would attend high school.

Work in the mines was hard and dangerous. For three years, he spent his days in the dark caves within the mining colony of Ciudanovița, working several kilometers underground using high-pressure water to mine the uranium, which meant he was soaking wet his entire shift. Day in and day out, he breathed in the fine dust of the radioactive ore and radon, a radioactive gas that's known to cause cancer and a number of other health issues.[1]

Perhaps this work fueled his hate for communism. Many workers in these mines felt exploited, not only by the work itself but also its implication in the broader government quest for economic growth at all costs. Individuals, communities, and the environment were part of that cost, and my father must have felt like a disposable tool for communism.[2] Many uranium miners would go on to die in their fifties, usually from lung cancer or leukemia.

Eventually, my father graduated high school, quit the mine, and moved to Timișoara to attend college. Under communism, higher education was covered by the government if a student passed the various sorting measures needed to place in a good institution, including earning high grades and test scores. If a student did especially well in high school, as my father did, the government also provided a *bursă*, a stipend that was meant to sustain a student's basic needs during college, including food and shelter. But it wasn't a generous amount, so my father had to work on top of his studies.

During his time studying in the university, he would visit his parents and siblings—but if he was a black sheep before, his color only deepened as he continued his studies. His older brothers and sisters had done well

---

1 For more information, see: Adrian Mogos and Michael Bird, "Soviet uranium legacy blights eastern EU," *euobserver,* March 15, 2016, https://euobserver.com/investigations/132406; and: Centers for Disease Control and Prevention, The National Institute for Occupational Safety and Health, "Worker Health Safety Studies—Uranium Miners," 2000, https://www.cdc.gov/niosh/pgms/worknotify/uranium.html#:~:text=Uranium%20Miners%20were%20exposed%20to,to%20the%20U.S.%20general%20public

2 Dacinia Crina Petrescu, Ruxandra M. Petrescu-Mag, and Ancuta Radu Tenter, "The Little Chernobyl of Romania: The Legacy of a Uranium Mine as Negotiation Platform for Sustainable Development and the Role of New Ethics," *Journal of Agricultural and Environmental Ethics* 32, no. 1 (February 2019), DOI:10.1007/s10806-019-09766-3

for themselves financially, not so much with salaries or cash, but with properties and livestock. Since collective property ownership never reached the farmland of Globu Craiovei, the communist government never took public ownership of their property. Still, even though they were doing well financially, none of them helped with his schooling or living expenses. And despite the fact that they were much more well off than my father, he carried an air of superiority when he visited home. He was going to be somebody and do something big with his life. Unlike them.

This perspective of self-importance, it turns out, was an all-too-common theme for him. As mentioned previously, he had carried the same air around my mom's family when he had visited her in Brăila in their early dating years.

These interactions were the seeds of what would later become an inflated, false sense of grandeur that plagued him for the rest of his life.

My father graduated from the Polytechnic University of Timişoara the year I was born and walked across the stage in an old blue suit with the cuffs folded up to hide the frayed and worn fabric. Like his suit, his life was coming apart at the seams—and of his own doing too. He had estranged himself from my family long before that first visit that sent me to the hospital. By the time I started kindergarten, he was a shadow father I thought I'd never know; a person my gentle grandfather swore he'd kill if he ever laid eyes on him again because, in his words, he destroyed my mother's life through his absence during their brief marriage, their divorce, and his lack of involvement in my life. My mother could have had a happy life with a good husband, but he had stolen that from her. As my grandfather saw it, my father had ruined my mother for men, not because things had been good but because they'd been so terribly bad she couldn't imagine going through such heartache again.

In spite of my father's impact on our family, our day-to-day life was peaceful. Communism was still in its "relaxed" stage when I was in elementary school; not much had changed since my birth. Our family continued to mind our own business, so the government didn't bother us. Upward mobility was still somewhat accessible if one knew how to network effectively within the upper circles. Even so, there was continued encroachment on personal freedom, especially freedom of speech and public gatherings. Any speech that was critical of the government wasn't tolerated. People couldn't gather in any sort of demonstration.

While the government didn't officially ban religion, they continued to schedule rallies or required school activities on Sundays during known worship hours in an effort to prevent religious assembly. In our church there were three masses, so even if we missed our normal time, my family would go later in the day. At these government rallies, we'd listen to political leaders who had traveled from *Bucureşti*—Bucharest—or who had been sent by Ceauşescu, the Romanian president, and then we'd chant the propaganda fed to us by whoever was leading the rally. If these happened during school hours, we would file out of our classes to join the gathering and line the streets with flowers and slogans: "*Ceauşescu, România. Stima Noastră şi Mîndria.*" Ceauşescu, România. Our Respect and Pride.

Away from the watchful eyes of the Securitate, Romanians across the country—including our family—secretly listened to Radio Free Europe, an uncensored world radio station. There, we could hear what was really going on in the outside world, not just the censored propaganda fed to us by the communist government. The news inside Romania was twisted to favor the government, lifting up communist ideals and squashing individualism. The government didn't want us to own anything, not even our own thoughts.

Among those also listening was my father, a burgeoning dissident. He would have burned down every bridge he had to the country rather than conform. And eventually, he would.

3

THE GRAY

The violins and cellos increased their tension and the drums beat low and slow. As the heavy, burgundy-and-gold brocade curtain drew back, I leaned forward, straining to take in every detail from our seats in the back upper balcony. The theatre was dark around me, and I felt my mom's shape next to me, sitting upright and proper like always.

On stage, I watched the opening act of *Carmen* by Georges Bizet unfold before me: a town square in Seville, Spain, located just outside a cigarette factory; soldiers watching the townspeople walking to work and errands; and finally a young peasant woman from the countryside, Micaëla, who asks after a guard named Don José. The soldiers tell her she can wait for him there, but instead she leaves with plans to return. Later, Don José comes out to take his place as a guard and the men tease him about Micaëla. He admits he loves her.

Soon, a group of women exit the cigarette factory for a smoking break. They take long drags of their cigarettes and flirt with the men, among whom is Don José. Then Carmen saunters out of the factory, and all the men's eyes turn toward her. She is like a magnet, drawing the men toward her while she remains coolly detached. They clamor for her attention, asking when she will love them. But she only has eyes for Don José. "Love is a rebellious bird," she replies, and tosses Don José a flower, giving him a meaningful look before walking off stage.[3] After everyone leaves, Don José picks up the flower.

I leaned forward in my seat, taking in the magic of budding love and the wonder of opera. At nine years old, I was beginning to develop my own curiosity about relationships. What would happen between sweet Micaëla and the handsome Don José? Would Carmen's beauty and mysteriousness steal his affection?

Enraptured, I slid further toward the edge of my seat, taking in the dramatic rising love of Don José and Carmen, the futile attempt by Micaëla to reclaim her lover, the desperate breakup of the prime couple, and finally, Carmen's heartbreaking lines.

"Carmen will never give way! Free she was born, and free she will die!"[4]

Then Don José stabs her to death.

I drew in a sharp breath and looked helplessly at my mom, whose attention was on Don José being arrested and walked off stage. The curtain closed. My heart raced. Mom looked at me and said, "What did you think? Did you like it?"

I nodded my head as Mom gathered her purse from the floor. Theatregoers around us murmured their approval of the opera, wondering aloud about Carmen's death and Don José's willingness to kill someone he loved just because she wouldn't be with him. As I listened to their conversations, I felt a hand on my shoulder edging me forward to follow the other patrons filing out of our row, leading me through the now-lit theatre, down the stairs, and toward the coat check line.

My mom gripped my hand as we exited Theatre Maria Filotti and into the freezing nighttime air of Brăila. We walked, just the two of us, toward the bus stop to take the short ride back to our apartment, our breaths making

---

3 For more information, see "What to Expect from Carmen" from The Met Opera, https://www.metopera.org/globalassets/discover/education/educator-guides/carmen/carmen.14-15.guide.pdf; and Betsy Schwarm and Linda Cantoni, s.v. "Carmen," *Britannica*, May 4, 2023, https://www.britannica.com/topic/Carmen-opera-by-Bizet

4 http://www.columbia.edu/itc/music/NYCO/carmen/cesttoi.html

little spiraled puffs as we talked, my mom smiling down at me, me smiling up at her.

It was a special night, with the person I loved most in the world.

Reflecting on that evening now and the story of *Carmen*, I can't help but notice the shared theme in my mom's experience with love. Romantic love, for my mom, had always meant pain. She had been on exactly one date since my father, and it didn't go well, probably because she brought me on the date with her. When my grandma questioned bringing a child on a first date, my mom said, "Well, I come with this. You either like it or you don't." When the man didn't call again, she didn't seem bothered. My mom had been ruined for love because my father had been an uncaring husband and absent parent. She didn't trust men. My mom was young when they met—just eighteen— and the painful first few years of adulthood had scarred her.

In spite of my mom's painful relationship with my father, I knew romance didn't always end in pain. I saw what steady commitment looked like every day between my grandparents and between my aunt and uncle. We knew family friends and people at church and my classmates' parents who seemed completely content together, some even happy. Real love *was* possible without ending up lonely like Micaëla . . . or getting stabbed to death like Carmen.

Accurate or not, that play stayed with me long after that evening. And during each of the operas my mom took me to throughout my childhood, I watched the unfolding drama of love—the excitement, the pain, the loss. Each time, the music gripped me, the lovers intoxicated me, and my childhood mind spun around and around, taking in the characters and storyline, even if I didn't always fully understand the meaning of what I was watching.

Of course, my childhood brain also did not fully comprehend Bizet's message in *Carmen*, which was well beyond the scope of romantic love: that freedom is more important than life. Carmen was not so much a romantic character as a free character. One who smoked, was sexually uninhibited, and did things her way, outside societal norms. She valued freedom above all else. While the theme of personal freedom was beyond my understanding at nine, I resonated with her character. While I was a good kid, I felt connected to her rebelliousness.

She was fierce. Untethered. Willing to fight and die for *herself*. Not for a man. Not for a mission. Herself.

Given the highly curated cultural environment in communist Romania, this message of freedom was dangerous. But perhaps whatever government official approved this opera saw a different message: If you try to be free, you'll die.

I can't help but reflect with tenderness on my nine-year-old self, so naïve, so wide-eyed at the possibilities ahead of her. I did, after all, have everything ahead of me—and believed I could do and be anything I wanted. And isn't that how childhood should be: carefree, open, curious, trusting?

But as I reflect now, with knowing, with scars, I also see the seed of resilience being planted in the many cultural experiences my mom exposed me to over the course of my upbringing: theatre, opera, orchestra, concerts, art museums, violin lessons, a cappella tutoring. She enrolled me in sports: gymnastics, ballet, volleyball, and swimming. After the doctor finally removed my tonsils at age seven, I had sprouted, no longer plagued by the fever, nausea, and fatigue that had marked my earliest years but instead full of wild energy and passion, leaping into each activity my mom enrolled me in with fervor.

I was raised to see possibility, personal expression, and the results of hard work and practice. My mom taught me to embrace beauty, nature, music, and color. She sent me to summer camp for two weeks a year, where I cried from homesickness, and yet she still insisted I go back the following year to have the experience of being away and forming my own identity. She took me to a tailor and ensured that I was always dressed to a T, fashionable like her. While we didn't have a lot of money, I was rich in exposure and, even as a child, began developing an ability to speak and move about in circles well beyond my station—and in communist Romania, station was everything. Her support and love built my confidence. I believed I could and should be heard and seen, even in the upper echelons of Romanian society.

My mother's love planted itself fiercely and firmly, deep within the unseen layers of my consciousness. A layer of armor against the world.

When I look in my mind's eye at little Luissa, walking quietly and safely while holding her mom's hand, humming the tune to "Habanera" from

Carmen, trusting the universe and herself and all the people in it, heading home to the safety of a loving family home, I feel a tenderness toward her. I was held and loved, nurtured and supported, brought up to believe I was worthy. Years later, far beyond my family's safety, this foundation would make all the difference.

—

My childhood continued to be a blessed one, although the carefree life I enjoyed until about age ten would not last. As communism shifted, so did the country's economic state, including my own family's. And as I grew older, I was forced to take on more responsibilities as a Romanian citizen, including working in the fields each year during harvest.

One afternoon, while completing my work in the fields (I was fourteen years old and in the ninth grade), I began to feel the defeat of day after day of labor. It was nearing lunch, and my body was giving out. I grasped an ear of corn with both hands, twisted firmly and tugged. When it didn't budge, I twisted more, then tugged again. Sweat beaded at my hairline and my fingers ached. I twisted twice this time, tugged, and it finally released, knocking me slightly off-balance. Steadying myself, I tossed it into the large bucket next to me and moved to the next ear.

Around me, my classmates were also working the corn fields; others were working the onions, tomatoes, and peppers. My stomach wrenched with hunger—we'd been at this for hours and hadn't stopped for a break. I turned my concentration on the next ear and the next as my thoughts drifted away from the field, and to the walks my mom and I took most weekends.

Ever since I was a young child, we'd explored our town by foot, walking from our apartment to the Danube River boardwalk, where we'd stroll through the grassy riverbank. Mom taught me how to collect chamomile flowers for tea, gripping each blossom gently with two fingers and lifting the bud off the stem. We'd make our way to the boats docked along the river, pick one that looked inviting, and sit inside, looking out at the river, my fingers tapping playfully on the water just like the little legs of a water spider, while talking and laughing together.

So much laughter.

Once, a fisherman came while we were having our waterside chats. He greeted us, smiling as we sheepishly climbed out of his boat. We blushed at first, then laughed about that too.

Sometimes we'd wander the boulevards of Brăila, always ending up at one of the two most beautiful boulevards: Alexandru Loan Cuza or Emperor Carol. Cuza Boulevard was a two-lane street with cobblestone sidewalks on either side. It had a wide median with the biggest acacia and oak trees my young eyes had ever seen. The median also had a paved walking path that stretched all the way to the Danube River and was dotted with benches my mother and I would rest on, chatting about school or work or the last show we had attended. The other, Carol Boulevard, was wider. Instead of trees, the city had planted rose bushes: amazing, vibrantly colored, different species of roses. It was truly a butterflies' and bees' paradise and was meticulously maintained by the city's workers.

Because we were living under the watchful eye of communism, patrollers were everywhere we went. They kept order, making sure we didn't bother the rose bushes or disrupt our fellow citizens. But even as a "good" kid, I couldn't resist the urge to steal roses when they weren't looking. I'd swiftly slide my fingers past the thorns to a cold, smooth spot on the stem, pushing my thumb swiftly to break the flower clean. Sometimes, I'd need to twist and yank to get it off, always darting my eyes about, making sure the patrollers weren't looking. More than once, I cut my fingers on thorns, sucking the cut as I walked home. Then I'd present the rose to my mother, who would *tsk* me for breaking the rules—but her eyes belied the reprimand, revealing her pleasure at receiving such a beautiful gift. Her joy was motivation enough for me to make rose thievery a habit.

My attention snapped back to the field when I heard the tell-tale sound of steps cracking in my direction. The field monitor was making his way to me.

I looked down at my bucket. It was full to the brim, so I hoisted it up with both hands, resting the handle on my hip and straining to steady the weight, then walked in the direction of the large truck already overflowing with corn for animal feed. The monitor pushed through one of the rows of corn, looked at me with the bucket, and nodded.

"Break's almost here."

I nodded, relieved to know I would eat soon.

"Empty this quickly and hurry back so you can clear more before lunch."

I nodded again, ducking my head and hurrying, the handle of the bucket digging into my hip as I trudged through the row, corn stalks brushing my legs and arms. Once the field monitor had crossed to another row, I stopped and set my bucket down, breathing heavily, lifting my face up to the sky and closing my eyes. It was an overcast day, perfect for a day of work in the fields. Just as I lifted my face, a ray of light cut through the clouds and hit my temple. The familiar clang rang out. Lunch!

I hoisted my heavy bucket with both hands and fast-walked to the truck, where I set my bucket down for one of the men to lift and empty. With my now-light bucket in hand, I made my way over to my backpack and withdrew a paper bag, which held the lunch Bunica had made for me early that morning. I joined my friends on top of a large pile of old corn fodder next to the truck. As I ate, I wondered if I'd meet quota that day. Or if one of my classmates would slack off and we'd all have to work extra to make up for it. And then I groaned inwardly when I remembered this was only day three; we still had eleven and a half days to go.

Sitting on my perch atop the massive piles of corn we'd shucked for animal feed, I ate my sandwich with a dirt-streaked face and tired muscles, willing my body to reenergize for the second half of the workday. As I chewed, I looked out at the flat farmland and wished the weeks away.

For kids coming of age in communist Romania, working the fields was a staple of our childhood just as much as reading, writing, and arithmetic. After all, the government said we had to do our part to support the country, even as children. We found it amusing that on Labor Day holiday in communist Romania, the president declared that the most appropriate way to celebrate was through labor, not rest.

For two weeks to a full month each fall, we would board buses to the field at seven in the morning and harvest crops until about three, gathering peppers, onions, corn, tomatoes, and other produce by hand. We were assigned at least one row and given a daily expected metric; and would have to report the number of bushels we'd gathered at the end of each workday.

Every day, we would be assigned to pick different types of crops. The Communist Youth Union organizers leading these efforts would perform random checks of our work, either by sampling the produce we picked or walking the rows to ensure we weren't being sloppy. They inspected our work for quality and quantity: The buckets had to be filled fully to be properly counted and recorded under our names for reporting purposes. If they decided our work was subpar, we'd have to go back and rework the assigned row. And if any rows were found unharvested—even if they hadn't assigned it to anyone—the whole class would be required to clear it, extending our workday to about eight hours. At the end of each workday, exhausted, dirty, and aching from the labor, we'd pile onto the buses and slump in our seats, often silent the entire ride back to the school, where we'd then still have to walk home.

Of course, we never got to bring the produce home—we were working for the collective. At home, my mother would draw me a bath, and I'd sit in the bathtub, washing my hair slowly, my fingers loosening the dirt from my scalp, my muscles relaxing in the warm water. When I finally forced myself out of the water, I'd dress, walk to the dinner table, and try hard to engage in the conversation. My grandparents would ask about my day, my mom would wonder why the bus had gotten back so late, my cousin Dragoş, then seven, would grin up at me and say he couldn't wait to work in the fields like me. I didn't have the heart to tell him it wasn't fun—not at all. Each day I wanted nothing more than to escape the fields and be back in the classroom, learning about math and science, reading books, and spending time with my friends.

Each night during these long weeks, I'd heave myself to bed, fall asleep within minutes, and awake early with sore muscles and an itch to learn. But my education would have to wait. I had more corn to harvest.

—

Our work in the fields only lasted a couple of weeks a year, but communism seemed like it would last indefinitely. As a child of eleven, I didn't fully understand the growing intensity of everyday life the grownups around me were experiencing: the watchful eyes of the Securitate, tracking anyone perceived as a threat to the order of communism; how neighbors and friends reported each other to the Securitate; the drastic rations on food, electricity, and water that left many families hungry, cold, and dirty.

Under the dictatorial leadership of Nicolae Ceaușescu, Romania's economic situation was worsening. Ceaușescu was obsessed with paying off Romania's national debt and limiting reliance on foreign countries for importing goods. To free up more money to funnel toward debt repayment, he rationed everything he could from the Romanian people.

Relatively quickly, life became hard.

Anything imported from the West, including fruits and vegetables, was extremely expensive; at the same time, the government exported everything they could to make money to pay down our debt, which further limited access to food. Water was rationed to two hours in the morning and two hours at night, turned on at impromptu times. When water was on, the pressure wasn't enough to take a shower, so my family started taking baths, sharing the water because there wasn't enough hot water to drain and refill the tub. We'd bathe in order of age: me first, followed by my mom, then my grandmother, and finally my grandfather. Thankfully, my aunt, uncle, and cousin now lived separately, so our bath was only shared among four people instead of seven. When it was my turn to bathe, I had to get in, wash quickly, and get out so that the water would still be warm for the rest of the family.

Electricity and gas were also only on for two hours in the evening during weekdays and four hours a day on the weekends, again at random times. Heat was controlled by a central system during those few hours a day, meaning we could turn the heat off but not control the temperature. In the winter in Romania, the temperature outside drops below freezing, and the limited hours of heat were not enough to maintain comfort in our home. When the heat was on, I'd huddle near the white metal calorifier anchored on the wall, through which hot water would flow, heating the metal grates and the space around it. Most of the time, the hot calorifier was lukewarm, the water flowing through it not hot at all. Because of the low initial water temperature at the source and the distance traveled through pipes, the heat dissipated by the time it reached all the targeted households. It was hard to sleep during those winter nights—I would shiver in my bed, willing my teeth to stay still and my body to stop shaking so I could sleep.

In the scorching summer months, we would experience the opposite. Romania, much like all the countries under communism, had no access to air conditioning.

The rations on food, water, and basic utilities became so restrictive it felt like we were falling backward in time, into the Stone Age.

When the electricity and gas were on, the house was in action: My grandmother would cook and my mother would wash the dishes or do other housework. My grandfather would gather water into pots, pans, and buckets, which we would use for drinking, cooking, or the toilet. And I would complete my homework while I had light by which to read and study. But even when the gas was on, there was so little umph that it took fifteen minutes to heat a little pot of water for coffee. Everything was slow, which was especially frustrating because we didn't know when the government would switch the power and gas off again. The adults always seemed to be in an excruciatingly slow rush, hurrying to get as many things done as possible while simultaneously waiting . . . and waiting.

After I finished my studies, I would sometimes read—my favorite pastime, even if by gas lamp—or watch one of the two television channels available while my grandparents and mom bustled around me. I preferred the English shows with subtitles. On Tuesdays, I'd watch *BBC Television Shakespeare*, or the mystery series *Hercule Poirot* or *Sherlock Holmes*; on Saturdays and Sundays the programs ran in the afternoon, electricity permitting. There were shows about art and music; cartoons like *Tom and Jerry*; old comedy mini-series like *Stan și Bran* (Stan Laurel and Oliver Hardy), *Charlie Chaplin*, or *Bewitched*; French comedies with Louis de Funés; or westerns with John Wayne. Entertainment would always be accompanied with communist indoctrination before or after the shows. These indoctrinations would include news about the Soviet Union or news from București, traditional music with communist messaging, and recitations about communist principles.

While we were allowed curated entertainment, we were almost entirely cut off from true news about the rest of the world, and especially the West—except, of course, from Radio Free Europe, which many Romanians still listened to religiously. Those broadcasts included anti-communist messaging and news about what was going on outside of the Iron Curtain—the metaphorical barrier between the Soviet Union and the rest of the world. We were kept behind this ideological curtain by the government, which tried hard to prevent us from being Westernized, keeping out Western ideals and instead feeding in communist messaging through television, newspapers, schooling, rallies, and more.

Along with the impact on daily life, the utility rations had other unintended negative consequences. Because warm water wasn't flowing steadily in the winter, pipes began to burst. And because the gas was turned off centrally—and suddenly—people would often forget to close the gas valves to their stoves and ovens. So when the central switch was flipped on again, poisonous, flammable gas would fill kitchens and entire apartments. Smoking was common in Romania. The combination was deadly.

This happened in my neighborhood: Someone lit a cigarette, and the entire block line blew up, killing more than a hundred people.

The fire blazed in my mind for days.

Food was heavily rationed too. I was still in middle school in 1980 when my grandfather retired. As rations took hold, he returned to work part-time as a butcher at a friend's shop to make a little extra money and gain access to meat. Even with his help, meat for our family became hard to access, and when we did secure some, the quality was poor. Before the economic downturn, fish was considered the food of the poor in Romania, especially for the people who lived by the Danube River or the Black Sea; now it was a staple in every home, the main source of animal protein. Cheese was a little easier to procure because it was produced by the heavily taxed Romanian farmers, but we were only allowed a small amount per household, which was set and tracked by the government. It helped that my uncle, a veterinarian, was rising to the upper circles of communism, rubbing shoulders with people who had access to the best foods and products. He would bring home pastrami, eggs, milk, and other food staples, helping ensure we were well fed. We shared our surplus with our neighbors and family friends who were less fortunate and struggling. The hard times brought everyone closer together.

Thankfully, I'd outgrown my childhood sickliness once I had my tonsils removed. Not only did this bring my family more peace of mind, but with my persistent infections a distant memory, I wasn't as picky about food. So while the food quality was poor and the variety limited, at least I could eat.

Even with all these rations and limitations, my mother worked to give me every comfort she could. My grandparents protected my time, insisting that I study by the limited light or candlelight each evening; if my studies were complete, I was to rest. My number one job was school, they said. I needed to keep up my energy if I was going to become a doctor.

A doctor—at age eleven, my dream had become anchored, set, unshakeable. My family knew it, my teachers knew it, my classmates knew it, and I knew it: Deep, deep down within my soul, I believed with unwavering conviction that I, Luissa Vrâncuţa, would become a doctor.

There wasn't some profound experience that illuminated this knowing within me, though it probably had something to do with my childhood spent in medical offices, my mother worrying over me, the doctor dismissing her concerns as she pushed back, insisting something was wrong. It probably had to do with the nausea and infections that battered my little body all those years. They eventually removed my enlarged, bacteria-colonized tonsils. Numbed only by local anesthesia at age seven, I was strapped by the head and limbs to a metal chair, my mouth propped open with metal, wild-eyed as the doctor, wearing neither gloves nor mask, snipped out the abscessed offending tissue and stitched me up, and then with a broad smile proclaimed: "*Gata! Acum te vei face bine.*" Done! Now you will get well.

Later, she told my mother: "*Ce ţi-am spus, de mult trebuiau scoase.*" I told you a long time ago these *had* to be removed. Yes, the very same doctor who refused time and time again to remove my ongoing source of failure to thrive.

Tears rolled down my face that day from fear, and I blinked back at the doctor, studying her face, her eyes still crinkled above me. Years later, at age eleven, I'd reflect on that moment with wonder. While the surgery had been horrible, there was no arguing about the result: I became well. To be able to heal another human—*that* was the ultimate power.

But that power was not easy to obtain. Our communist system was set up so that only the best and brightest of us could become doctors—although sometimes that group of achievers included the children of people who were the most connected, even if they didn't qualify on their merits. From a young age, we were sorted by ability. Our smarts and talent were judged as we filtered into high schools based on our grades and testing abilities and then, if we performed well again, medical school. I had a lot of hoops ahead of me, the biggest one being medical school entrance exams.

This goal of becoming a doctor was grand. But I was raised to believe I was grand too. Our meager middle class communist existence, with the cold nights and bursts of gas and electricity and limited food and hard work in the fields and government control . . . well, those hardships were bearable to me, because in spite of it all, I was protected. Believed in. Supported. Cocooned from the worst of the hardships within the bubble of the love of my family. The golden child that would achieve her dream someday. The girl who would become a doctor, and whose family would know they'd done everything in their power to help her do it.

—

While my family and I grew accustomed to the hardships of everyday life in Brăila, my father was no longer in Romania. His budding dissidence in Timișoara had progressed to organized attempts to overthrow the communist government. When the Securitate were tipped off to his activities, he fled Romania, leaving on a little inflatable boat with his second wife and her child across the Danube River in the spring of 1976 (I was eight at the time). They were apprehended in Yugoslavia, where in such cases the Yugoslavian government would ask for ransom money to return defectors. Because of my paternal grandmother's Swedish roots, the German government offered a ransom for my father, and Germany outbid Romania.[5] My father lived one year in Germany before going on to the United States with his now-pregnant wife and stepdaughter. There, he declared political asylum and cut ties to Romania. My half-sister, Violet, eight years younger than me, was born in America.

He hadn't said goodbye, and I didn't miss him. But while my father had such a small role in my life, his actions produced a ripple effect of consequences for my family. My mom learned from some of her connections at work that our phone line was being recorded. I wasn't allowed to take English at school because the government was trying to prevent me from joining my father in the United States. When he called once per year or so, usually on my birthday, I knew to be careful about what I said, keeping the conversation light and positive about the situation in Romania.

Not that there was any depth to our conversations or in my relationship with my father. The last time I'd seen him, his third visit ever, was when I was in kindergarten.

That day, I was in class when the teacher came and whispered in my ear: "*Cineva a venit să te vadă.*" Someone is here to see you. She took me by the hand and led me along the hallway and through the big doors to the large entryway to the school. In the corner of the foyer, I saw a strange man looking expectantly at me. My teacher led me to him, and I looked up at her, confused, as she lifted me up and set me on the wooden credenza in front of the man. I sat, blinking up at the two adults, one I knew and the other I didn't.

I stared at him: dark mustache, black suit with thin white stripes, white shirt, light blue tie. Then I recognized who it was from the few pictures I'd seen growing up. "The Dog"—that's what my family called him at home. A nobody who abandons his family. An animal who wanders off, who doesn't take care of his child.

---

5   Had my father been returned to Romania, he would likely have been thrown in prison for a long sentence as an enemy of the state. Such sentences often meant forced labor in projects like the building of the Danube-Black Sea Channel. Incidentally, that project in particular was considered to be a surreptitious way of disposing of political dissidents without violating the terms of the Geneva Convention.

"*Tati e aici,*" he said. Daddy's here.

My teacher looked from me to him and back to me. I eyed him but said nothing.

"*Uite ce ți-am adus.*" Look what I brought you. He reached into his jacket and withdrew a burgundy fountain pen with a silver cap. I studied it without speaking, recognizing the gold tip.

"*I-al,*" he said. Here. "*Asta ți-a adus tati.*" This is what Daddy brought you. He smiled and held it out to me to take.

"*Nu vreau,*" I replied. I don't want it. My voice was flat as I continued in Romanian, "*Mami are unul la fel. Nu îl vreau pe al tău.*" My mom has one like that. I don't want yours.

He stared at me, the pen suspended midair. His smile dropped as he looked at my teacher with lifted eyebrows. When his gaze returned to me, he looked angry.

Then he placed the pen back in his jacket, turned around, and left. I leaned forward on the credenza, my palms on the cool wood, and stared down at my dangling feet as the door to the school swung open and then click-clicked shut. I heard my teacher draw a quick breath, then lean over to pick me up and set me on the ground.

I hadn't seen him since. No, there was no depth to our relationship. Not then. Not ever.

Still, I looked forward to his call each year. He was, after all, my father. As I grew older, I wanted to know him more—this man who had spent his entire life away from me, a father but not really. While I felt whole and complete with the family I had, doesn't every young girl wish to know her father?

In spite of the recorded line, the absence, the surface-level conversation, how his decisions impacted our family, I answered his call every year and spoke politely, wondering if I'd ever see him again.

4

AVE, PADRE

I sat in the weathered tan chaise lounge in the church office, eyeing the almanac of anatomy book my best friend, Stella, had given me for my birthday. Stella and I called each other "Bîzu," a Romanian word for a buzzing bee. After just a few months of ownership, the cover was already worn at the corners, the pages supple from use. I flipped to the page about muscles, studying the parts of the body, willing my brain to memorize the many facts I'd need to recall in order to pass my tests later that year.

Sternocleidomastoid. Intercostals (external and internal). Diaphragm. Erector spinae (sacrospinalis). Splenius capitis et cervicis.

Reaching into my bookbag, I pulled out a notebook and pencil and carefully began drawing the image: outlining the head, neck, shoulders, arms, torso, hips, legs, feet. Then I drew lines, copying the words on the diagram carefully, saying each word aloud as I wrote it. I was engrossed in this task when the door creaked open behind me. Twisting in my chair, I saw Padre, our parish priest, walk toward me, stopping in front of me to crane his neck and peer down at my beloved book.

"Studying again?"

I nodded. "I have to if I'm to become a doctor."

Padre smiled in his deep, joyous way as he made his way slowly but purposefully toward his desk, pausing to look out of his window onto the church courtyard. The contrast of his silhouette in the window struck me: his tall, broad frame and dark hair set against the whiteness beyond, where winter had made its mark on the church grounds. Then my gaze adjusted to take in his presence: scrutinizing deep-green eyes guarded by bushy eyebrows. Warm face, even when trying to make a serious point, which always made me feel at home. Large hands—more like a field worker's than a priest's—which would pat my head when I needed a cheer-up, a nudge, or a scold.

Padre settled into his broad leather chair, met my eyes, and smiled.

"Back to work then," he said, settling in behind his wide mahogany desk. "For both of us."

He motioned to the stack of papers piled neatly to his left, another stack of unopened letters just above them.

"Might take me all afternoon."

I grinned and shifted in my chair, settling in for another long day in Padre's office.

He slid open a drawer in his desk, retrieved his eyeglasses, sighed purposefully as if steeling himself for the pile before him, and lifted the first paper, examining it closely before writing something and moving it to the right of his desk.

I looked back down at my partially completed drawing, contemplating the intricacy of the human body, which I was supposed to be an expert on in just a few years' time. I would be treating this body: healing it, helping it. But first, I needed to understand it. And I needed to pass the test to get into medical school. I continued labeling.

Semispinalis. Multifidus. Rotatores.

Every so often I glanced up at Padre, studying his serious expression—brow furrowed, eyes focused, head down; writing or reading. When I looked at him, I didn't just see a priest—the most revered person in our Catholic community, the individual every parishioner turned to in times of need or want. I didn't simply see the man separated from the rest of us by his commitment to God or the person who had dedicated his life to rebuilding our church, Parohia Romano-Catolică Brăila, as it was officially named. Every Catholic church has a patron and ours was dedicated to the Virgin Mary, specifically to Her Ascension to heaven.

While our church was named after the Virgin Mother, I saw Padre as a Father but also as a father.

Now seventeen, I'd spent the last seven years learning from, and leaning on, Padre. Something drew us to each other, a relationship that felt like a parental bond. He was my Catholic priest and the father figure I needed. Padre was instrumental in my life.

Growing up, I hadn't felt pain from the absence of my father, but I still noticed the gap where a dad should have been. While my mom, grandfather, and grandmother created a charmed ring around me of love, security, and support, every young girl needs an active, loving male presence in her life. My grandfather filled an important fatherly role, but he was too old to fully step into the role of father. Plus, he was busy—always working to provide for us. I loved him dearly but I needed more than he could offer as a father figure. Padre was almost exactly a year older than my own father, their birthdays just one year and one day apart, and his entire world revolved around being available for his congregation.

I met Padre during one of his yearly household visits when I was around seven years old. Each spring, he would make his rounds to all the families' homes in the congregation to break bread and bless the household. When he arrived at our house, I took in his kind eyes and dark features; he was tall, with broad shoulders, solid-built leaning toward heavyset, and he seemed seven feet tall because of the way my family revered him. As we sat around the table enjoying the meal my grandmother had prepared, I wriggled uncomfortably in my Sunday dress, my mind on things I'd rather be doing: gymnastics, reading, playing my violin. My mother sat next to me, my grandfather and grandmother across the table, and Padre at the head of the table, the seat of honor. When the conversation lulled, Padre looked at me.

"We need to talk about first communion," he said.

I groaned inwardly as I poked at the food on my plate. First communion meant classes—a lot of them, two to three times a week for a full month. A full month of listening, studying, and getting quizzed during the Easter Lent season, sometimes before, sometimes after the already lengthy masses, with parents sitting in the pews scrutinizing our every move and response. At my age, a month sounded like an eternity! And then there was the ceremony itself: dressing up in a fluffy white dress and attending a long, special mass where I'd have to wait quietly in the pew for what seemed like hours before taking the sacrament for the first time. There would be a party of some sort with my family, so at least there would be cake. But still, there was no way I could do all my schoolwork and extracurriculars while also completing the preparation for first communion.

Without looking up, I knew four pairs of eyes were locked on me. I slid my gaze to Padre and then lifted my chin.

"I don't have time for that," I finally said. "I'm busy doing gymnastics."

My mother let out a soft "oh" next to me. My grandmother's eyebrows lifted. My grandfather cleared his throat.

Padre, to his credit, didn't argue his point. The conversation shifted and I said a polite goodbye at the end of the evening, then rushed to the living room to switch on the television. While my family didn't scold me that night—in fact, Bunicu chuckled softly later that evening and winked at me—I knew my response hadn't gone over well. Everyone knows one does not talk back to the priest.

Padre "forgot" to stop by our house the next spring.

My mom didn't forget to enroll me in first communion classes, though. I attended every single one.

Despite our bumpy start, Padre must have appreciated something about my fierce spirit, because by the time I was about ten, our relationship evolved from chatting at church to long conversations in his office, reading or talking about life. Church also became a central part of my world: I attended mass on Sundays and Tuesdays, and once I joined the church choir, I was at the church on Wednesdays and Fridays too. In choir, I sang a cappella, stationed directly next to the organ, which was played by a sometimes-mean nun, Sister Maria. She looked mean too: small, thin frame, stern expression, furrowed forehead, squinting steel-blue eyes, pursed thin lips. Her gray hair was always covered by a *basma*, a kerchief; her clothes conformed to a strict color palette of gray, white, and black.

During choir practice, Sister Maria would stare at the sheet music through her soda-bottle-thick glasses as her fingers moved gracefully along the keys, her voice surprisingly angelic and powerful. I sang with her, my song a prayer because I never could learn to pray like the rest of my peers. I was too fidgety and couldn't concentrate long enough to talk to God in my head. So I sang with my voice and my heart, joining the chorus of my peers and Sister Maria, lifting my words up to heaven. It was during these many weeks of singing and attending church that my relationship with Padre deepened, the inner longing for a parental male figure pulling me toward him after practice and mass. Looking back, these months and years strengthened my spirituality, creating inner peace I would lean on during difficult years to come.

Along with appreciating Padre as a personal father figure, I admired him for who he was and how he led our church. He was funny and serious, strict when he had to be, but also naturally warm and kind. He was smart: a scholar of the Bible and a polyglot who spoke Italian, German, and Hebrew. His sermons were well put together, he never read from a paper, and he always taught in stories that kept the interest of everyone in mass, even the kids. During homilies, he would walk down the aisle and talk to us like he was having a personal conversation with each parishioner, just like I imagined Jesus would do.

Church members respected Padre for his impact on the community. When he'd arrived at our church years earlier, the church had been in shambles, falling apart and desperately needing maintenance. The congregation was waning. Catholicism in Romania was not strong, especially since the communist party didn't support religious gatherings. But Padre had a plan to revive the building and congregation. He was handy and strong-willed: Not only did he work relentlessly to obtain the funds and get approvals from both the archbishop and the local government, but he also painted the building inside and out; restored furniture, sculptures, and frescas; installed Carrera marble floors; added ambient lighting; and worked the grounds and gardens. He used his skills to fix the church both literally and metaphorically, bringing together the members with his light and energy, restoring the building and its people. The sanctuary became a small oasis for the soul and the body.

He earned respect not just from us but from the Vatican too. Once or twice a year, he'd travel to Vatican City to meet with *Papa*, the Pope. He'd come back from these trips with gifts for us kids, often candy, scarves, or trinkets, and pass them out with the biggest smile on his face—and on ours.

My father had only ever gifted me a piece of candy, the kind you get for free during a flight, and the fountain pen I refused.

Over time, I started going to Padre with my preteen woes and, eventually, teenage challenges: school, friends, boys. He began inviting me to his second-floor office. I'd either read or study while he worked, or we'd have conversations about life, sitting across from each other at a round table in his office. Sometimes I'd sit on the chaise lounge while he pulled one of the chairs from the table over to me. We talked about everything, and he sat patiently while I laughed, vented, and cried. Each time, he'd listen quietly until I was done talking and then soften his advice with jokes.

When I was upset with a friend from school, he would say: "You have choices, you know. You can stay mad . . . but what good will that do? You will frown, look ugly, and get old faster. Or you can talk things over while taking a walk. Afterwards, you both should go for ice cream. I tell you, nobody can remain serious while eating ice cream. Nobody."

When I was worried about an upcoming test: "Do you think you studied enough? If no, then what are you waiting for? Go study! If yes, then worrying is a sign of self-doubt. Don't doubt yourself. Remain confident and believe."

When I was swooning over my first boyfriend, Walter: "Don't be silly, OK?"

I wasn't totally sure what he meant by "silly," but I figured it had something to do with Walter's kiss a couple weeks earlier. Of course, I hadn't told Padre that Walter had kissed me already. And anyway, being a good Catholic, I had already asked Walter not to kiss me again.

Even at seventeen, I was innocent to the world and thought I could get pregnant just from a kiss. I was raised not to talk about sexuality and certainly to avoid anything even mildly sexual. Sex was taboo. A sin, not just in the Catholic Church but also within communism.

We had no sex education in school, and the prevailing advice was to wait until our wedding night and we'd find out all we needed to know. Kissing, cuddling, or any kind of physical touch was all off-limits. Sex was a mysterious land I didn't venture into, even in private conversation with my friends. Padre didn't need to worry about me.

Looking back, this attitude was not healthy or prudent. Knowledge is power. And besides, when something is forbidden, even in conversation, it becomes more intriguing. On the other hand, when things are explained openly, the mystery is unveiled. You see into possible outcomes like sexually transmitted infections and unwanted pregnancy and how these might affect future goals—and, at the same time, you see sex is just a part of life. Opening up the conversation is always a wise thing.

But back then, I didn't have this awareness. All I knew was that Walter kissed me and he was not to do it again.

When I brought Walter up again the following week, Padre crinkled his bushy eyebrows, looked straight into my eyes and, with his fatherly smile, reminded me, "I told you, don't be silly."

A father protects and cares for his daughter. He warns her away from harm. He counsels her when she's struggling or stuck or upset. He celebrates with her when she's happy. That's what Padre did for me. Who he was for me. A Father and a father.

As Padre continued to be a staple in my life, so was God. My mom had a complicated relationship with religion when I was younger, refusing to attend church or take the holy sacrament. She couldn't understand why God hadn't been there for her during the destruction of her marriage, when she had needed Him most. But as I entered my teens, and, I think, as the wounds from my father began to heal, she made her peace with God and renewed her relationship to Catholicism. She became a steadfast member of the congregation, never missing mass. Later on, upon my departure from Romania, she picked up praying her rosary daily.

Every Sunday of my later childhood was a holiday ritual: We'd sleep in late and attend mass, followed by a big family dinner in our small apartment with my mom, grandparents, uncle, aunt, and cousin. We'd pull the table into the living room and enjoy the three-course meal prepared by the women with simple ingredients and a lot of love, and we'd talk about the sermon, life, and more. I would look around the table and feel warm. Loved. By my family, my church, and my Father-father. Afterward, we would enjoy coffee and a siesta or watch the afternoon TV program, followed by getting ready for school on Monday.

Life seemed so simple. Clear. Like the path before me would always remain. I was to love and honor my family and God. I was to keep my head down within the communist system around me, follow the rules, and do my best to build the right relationships in the upper circles. I was to study hard and become a doctor. I was to trust that God had a plan, that He would never give me more than I could handle. That there is a reason for every cross we must bear in this world, that the seasons of famine produce seasons of rich harvest, that good Catholics take on the suffering they're given because, in suffering, we are made better. Worthy. Holy.

I was to trust that if I followed the rules of the government and church, and took on hardships with grace, life would work out exactly as I desired.

—

Life "working out" included becoming a doctor, and my dream hinged on navigating the Romanian school system. At seventeen, I was nearing the fateful testing date, when I'd take the exam that would determine my destiny. I wasn't worried. Not only did I believe in my own intelligence and ability, thanks to the encouragement from my family, but I also knew I had done the work. Along with the formal studying I'd done for several months, I had absorbed everything I could about medicine and the body since fifth grade, the year I'd decided on this path. I'd studied the almanac of anatomy Bîzu had gifted me, learning about Leonardo da Vinci's drawings of the human form and memorizing the Latinate terms, which came easily for me after taking one year of Latin in my last year of middle school. I'd competed in the city-wide Biology Olympiad and won first place, grinning from the stage at my mom, grandparents, aunt, uncle, and cousin, all cheering me on from the audience as I accepted my trophy. I had pored over science books when I should have been doing homework, curled up on the couch when the electricity was on each evening.

I couldn't help myself. I was drawn to the human body and the anatomy of how things work. Physics was too abstract for me. It's just electricity or a fork or a fulcrum. I was interested in hearts and capillaries and cells.

The body was like a puzzle. When I started studying physiology, and learning how things work, I was amazed at how the heart pumps the blood to the lungs and through the body. At how every organ and system had its own precise task to fulfill again and again. At the exchange of oxygen and carbon dioxide in the capillary beds.

I was stunned by the intricacy of the human system, with everything thought of, nothing left to chance. The human body is such a beautiful piece of art, even when just considering a piece of it, like the arm: the biceps, the veins, the forearm, the fingers. God or evolution, I wasn't sure, but I knew the interworking of the human body was awe-inspiring—a perfect system.

As a doctor, I would get to devote my life to the work of art and science that is the human body.

Plus, I had a knowing within me, an unshakeable calling that felt like destiny. Of course I would become a doctor. It was the only path I could choose. But there were many others who wanted to pursue the same path, people I would be in competition with for a coveted spot in medical school. In fifth grade, the year I anchored to my dream, there were ten other kids—seven girls, three boys—who professed the same dream.

While I believed in myself and my dream, I still had to jump through all the hoops of the Romanian system. The truth was, we'd be lucky if even one of the eleven of us dreamers in my fifth-grade class achieved our shared goal. I was determined that it would be me.

Competition for medical school was especially intense because of the value placed on higher education in Eastern Europe, and especially in Romania. The pursuit of academic excellence was almost like the pursuit of holiness in religion. Being a doctor or lawyer back then was considered a noble achievement. Reaching that professional level requires years of academic success and dedication, starting from a young age.

Even in fifth grade, the sorting had already begun. We were judged based on our grades and test scores, and depending on how we did throughout our budding academic careers, we'd eventually end up at one of three tiered high schools. Before graduating middle school, we took an exam that classified where each of us would go to high school. A friend of mine, Maria, was sorted into a textiles class, placed at a high school with a textile track, and students would spend a half-day per week learning the trade they would need later on to work in a textile factory. When she told me, I remember a dull feeling in my gut, because I knew what that meant for her.

Her destiny was determined as a teenager—by the government.

There is no shame in working a factory job. But in Romania during that time, life was hard for people in manual labor jobs, and it was demeaning to be placed in such a profession. Factory workers were known for walking around in threadbare clothing, and the work was considered the lowest profession one could enter. Everything in Romania was centered on education and getting into the right school. If you didn't do well with academics, you wouldn't fit into society. I heard the remarks about such placement, both from my family and within the community, and knew that sorting into a trade school would be a black mark on my family. There was no professional upward mobility in communism—if I was placed in a trade high school, I would never rise. I would be destined to a life of hardship and poverty. There were no options outside of education, and no future if you didn't study hard and test well. As such, parents and grandparents were obsessed with education for their progenies. Education equaled status—no ifs, ands, or buts.

What made this system especially unfair is that there were only a limited number of slots per professional track. So if we had thirty-six kids in a class, for example, only twelve could go to the top tier, the electronics track; twelve could go to the second tier, the mechanics track; and twelve could go to the third tier, the technical track. A child could be right on the line between any of those sorting groups, and could be fully capable of their dream profession, but if their test scores weren't high enough to make it into the government-determined group of twelve, their fate was forever sealed.

Unless, of course, you had a family member in the upper ranks of the communist party. Children of party members, even those who weren't performing in school, seemed to magically move through the top-ranking tiers. This further, and unfairly, increased the competition for top spots.

In the Romanian system, a student had to be placed into the electronics/math/physics track with a very rigorous exact sciences curriculum to go on to medical school. From there, a future doctor would continue straight to six years of medical school, unlike the United States system, where students complete a four-year degree first, take the MCAT, and then apply to medical schools.

So it was a relief when I received my middle school test results and was placed into the electronics class of Nicolae Iorga, the second-best high school in Brăila at the time, a path that enabled me to eventually take the test for medical school. I knew I'd need to absorb and memorize everything I could about human anatomy, physics, and chemistry if I was to pass the rigorous, competitive testing required to be admitted.

The entrance exam in Romania was administered in July of every year—and once a year only. Since as many as fifteen to twenty students competed for each spot, competition was intense. Admission to medical school was granted to the students who scored highest on the placement test; once a set number of slots were filled, no more students were admitted. The line was drawn and our futures were determined. The total number of annual slots was allocated by the Ministry of Education, and winning students were dispersed to the universities with medical schools, located in București, Iași, Timișoara, and Cluj-Napoca.

One plus of our education system was that everything was free—or at least we had already paid for it through heavy taxation under communism. Once I passed my medical school entrance exams, and I was certain I would, I would receive a full education as a doctor without paying one *leu*. If a student didn't pass, they had the option of waiting a year to take the exams again or beginning work in another field.

Because of the immense importance of this sorting, most Romanian families, including mine, would never dream of having their children work, even on the weekends to earn a little spending money. Aside from the few weeks a year of forced work in the fields, our entire lives were concentrated on studying. So my family's doting continued, and they allowed me to focus solely on my studies, to exercise my mind instead of helping around the house, working, or taking on regular chores. I knew they were sacrificing so I could focus and therefore took my time seriously, studying for hours each day and meeting with a chemistry tutor twice a week and a physics tutor once a week. Anatomy came easy to me, so I studied on my own. While I did meet up with friends and occasionally visit with relatives, most of my life revolved around keeping a tight focus on this goal. Nothing mattered more than excelling in school and studying so I could get high marks on the medical school entrance test. There was no other route to my dream. Like they say, I had my "eyes on the prize."

Becoming a doctor would also enable upward social and economic mobility for my family. Their future and mine would be determined by my ability to score high on the exam. My friends, extended family, and Padre believed in me. I believed in me. Failure, especially in communist Romania, was not an option.

—

The months went on, and in June of 1986 I had graduated high school and was in the final weeks of prep before the test. My weeks consisted of studying, church, studying, music lessons, studying, catching a movie with friends, and studying. And then more studying. Nothing mattered more than doing well on that one test. My entire future hinged on its success.

But while I felt a lot of pressure, I also felt confident that I would earn my spot in medical school. I knew I'd done the work, that I was bright enough, and that my future was already written: I would become a doctor.

When it finally came time to take the entrance test, I was ready. We took the seven-hour train to Timișoara; we had decided I should attend medical school there since we had family in the city. We spent the night at Aunt

Katerina's. The following morning Mom and I took the bus to the university where the test was to be administered. I tried to distract myself from my anxiety jitters by staring at the dew of the summer morning still hugging bus windows and tree leaves.

The ride felt brief. When we stepped off the bus, Mom hugged me, wished me well, then watched me go through the large entrance doors of the red brick building. She would return later on and wait outside the building until I finished my test. Standing outside the door of the testing room, with only blank paper and pencils in my hand, I felt a mix of concern and confidence. Concern because I knew the impact this one test would have on my life; confidence because I'd been studying practically my whole life. I was readier than ready.

The test was a blur, and it felt like no time before I was back outside those same doors, more confident than when I'd entered. I knew I hadn't gotten 100 percent, but I was certain I'd done well enough to rank in the top group and be admitted into medical school. Now I just had to wait for the tests to be graded and ranked, and to be notified by mail that I'd be going to medical school in the fall.

The next day we took the train back to Brăila. I'd thought I would feel relieved that this test was behind me, but instead I spent the long train ride in the company of self-doubt, trying to go back over each test question and my answer. By the time I got home, I was exhausted by the mental tug-of-war and was convinced I had gotten none of the answers right.

I distracted myself over the next two weeks by keeping even busier than normal. I threw myself into songs for the church choir, lifting my eyes to heaven and voice to the congregation while I sang. I attended communist-approved dollar movies at the Cinema Central with friends—often old westerns with John Wayne or films from India with Raj Kapoor—and we walked to the park near the promenade afterward, strolling underneath the big clock, a landmark of downtown Brăila. I attended the theatre with my mom, breathing in the drama on stage, the song, the rise and fall of emotions in a two-hour play. I read, this time for fun, escaping reality with books like *Anna Karenina*, *Crime and Punishment*, and *War and Peace*. I sank into

Eminescu's "*Luceafărul*," or "The Evening Star," a long, beautiful poem about a princess who falls in love with the immortal star *Luceafăr*, who, sharing her love, takes the human form and attempts to become mortal; that I reread over and over. I tried my best not to think about my test making its way to the processing centers, the tally being taken, a letter being written, a stamp being applied, and an envelope containing my entire future making its way toward Brăila and into our mailbox.

Finally, the day came.

When I checked the mail and saw the envelope I'd been waiting for, I carried it up the stairs to our apartment and set it on the dining table, waiting for my grandfather to arrive from the part-time job he'd taken post-retirement to procure meat for us. The afternoon passed with excruciating slowness, but I couldn't open it without him. I sat at the table and tried distracting myself with reading but kept casting anxious glances toward the envelope and picturing myself in a white coat, wearing a name badge that read: Dr. Vrâncuța. Yes, that sounded just right.

My destiny waited for me in that envelope. Surely I would be preparing to go to medical school that very night.

When I heard the metal click of the doorknob and my grandfather's heavy feet stepping inside, I called out to him.

"*Bunicule! A venit scrisoarea.*" Grandfather! The letter came.

I heard the drop of a bag on the floor, and my grandmother's and mom's fast footsteps from the living room. I retrieved the envelope and stood waiting for them, clutching the thin paper with the thin letter holding grand hope for my family's future. My grandfather looked almost out of breath by the time he made the short walk into the kitchen, my grandmother and mom hurrying in behind him.

"*Deschide-o!*" my grandfather said. Open it! I looked up at him standing in front of me. His face was overtaken by a nervous smile and his eyes crinkled when they met mine. His voice softened and he placed a hand on my shoulder. "*Deschide-o.*"

I heard my mom's and grandmother's feet shuffle on the stone floor as they moved closer. My heart sounded in my ears and my fingers trembled as I sat down, slid my finger under the envelope, and pulled the paper out, unfolding once, twice.

Reading the letter. *No, not possible.*

Reading it again.

My heart louder. My breath fast. My mom's warm breath on the top of my head as she hovered over me to read it too. The hushed sound of her voice as she said to me in Romanian, "You'll try again next year."

I looked up at my mom, my grandmother, my grandfather. Their forms blurred as tears filled my eyes and slowly rolled over my lashes and down my cheeks. My chest, full of anticipation of this moment, finally had no more power to hold it all in. I felt like I was collapsing inward, my ribs constricting, my pulse racing. Thoughts rushed through my head but nothing made sense. I was overcome: anguish, disappointment, sadness, revolt. Now what? *Da capo al fine.* From the beginning to the end. Again. All I wanted in life was to make them proud. How had this happened? How had I failed at the one thing that was my destiny?

I had never failed before. Not once.

As a singer, I had been given solos. As a student, I was known by teachers for excellence in homework and testing. As a gymnast, I had been asked to join the Olympic training team. Even as a Catholic and Romanian citizen, I had followed God, always staying chaste and pure, always doing everything my church, family, and the regime asked of me. I was disciplined, driven, determined.

And yet . . . I had failed?

I will have to start all over again, I thought, the paper still in my hands. The studying, the test prep, all of it. I was supposed to be going to medical school but instead I would be retaking a test I had been so sure I'd done well on.

And what if I failed again? What if I didn't ever make it into medical school?

I reminded myself that I hadn't had a lot of time to immerse myself in studying. High school had ended in June and I took the test about two weeks later. Plus, school was intense until the bitter end of our high school studies, so we didn't have the luxury of time to focus solely on exam prep.

Sitting at the table, my family silent around me, I took in my mom's words. She was right. With so much time to prepare this time, I knew I could do well. I would take the test again in a year. Between now and then, I would study every day. I would work with more tutors. I would apply myself rigorously to my dream. Yes, that's what I would do.

Wiping away my tears, I looked up at my mom with a sad smile, my grandfather's heavy hand and the weight of my family's future still on my shoulder.

"*Îl voi da din nou la anul,*" I said, my Romanian dripping with hope but weighted in pain. I'll take it again next year. "*Voi încerca din nou.*" I will try again.

—

And so, studying became my life. The next morning, I took out the textbooks I'd set aside during the weeks-long wait for my test results and created a plan for myself, making notes about what I recalled about the test so I could study strategically. There were no study guides or test prep classes back then. All I could do was memorize material from my medical books, studying obsessively from cover to cover, and hope I chose the right material to focus on. I had roughly a year to learn everything I could about the human body, physics, and chemistry, and I would apply myself faithfully so that the next time I tested, I would be in.

The second test, I knew, was my last shot. There would be no third test in communist Romania. A second failure would mean a different destiny. Failure was not an option.

I began studying obsessively, even bringing my books to the dinner table. My mom made calls, gathering recommendations for tutors in chemistry and physics, the two subjects I was competent in but guessed may have been my weak areas on the test. I would work with tutors four days a week, two days in chemistry and two in physics, and study my books in between. During these sessions, we would focus solely on the material, not on how to take standardized tests, because test-taking strategies were not yet taught in Romania. In a little under a year, I reasoned, I would be ready for the next exam.

As the weeks went on, though, I couldn't help but wonder if my test scores hadn't actually been the reason I wasn't admitted to medical school.

The rejection letter I received hadn't provided any details about my test or ranking within the pool of applicants. I wasn't given any information about my percentages in each test subject or even the overall score. When I'd left the testing center, I had felt good, certain that I'd done well. I had known most of the answers and only struggled with a handful. Of course, it was possible there were brighter students in the room that day. There were only five medical schools in a country of 22 million, after all. Maybe there just weren't enough spots for all of us who did well.

It was also true that in our communist society, it wasn't always the best and brightest that prevailed but instead often the most connected. If a higher-up had a son or daughter among the pool of test-takers, chances were their kid would be in, regardless of the skill, talent, or test scores. All the higher-ups had to do was make a phone call. Maybe there had been too many phone calls made . . . and I had been bumped.

While I couldn't be sure of the reason, it didn't matter anyway. I couldn't change communism. The only thing I could control was my preparation. I needed to be the best next time. Not in the top scores—*the* top score.

Achieving this goal was made more difficult by the testing format. There were no multiple-choice questions; instead, tests were entirely in essay format. This highly subjective exam style required me to not only be expertly versed in the material but to also know how to write a well-formed essay, quickly.

Over the next months, I kept my head down, only taking breaks from studying for family, church, and my new boyfriend, Paul.

Around the first of the year, nearly five months after receiving my rejection letter, I was sitting at the kitchen table with my tutor when the phone rang during one of the day's stretches of electricity. I ignored it, drawing the Krebs cycle from memory and hovering over a blank spot I just couldn't recall. I knew it was related to Acetyl-CoA, a molecule involved in biochemical reactions in the body. I stared at the empty spot on the page as my mom answered with a polite *bună ziua,* good day. When silence stretched in the space behind me, I glanced over my shoulder toward my mom, whose expression was drawn tight.

She pulled the phone away from her ear, the cord in the wall swinging as she stretched it out to me. Her voice was stilted as she said, "It's your father."

My tutor left the room, heading toward our front door to take a break outside, and Mom handed me the phone. I held it up to my ear, the hard plastic cold against my skin. My mom sat down in the tutor's seat, her right palm flat on her left bicep, her thumb unconsciously rubbing the fabric on her sleeve as she stared at me.

"*Bună ziua*," I said, echoing my mother.

"*Este tati*," he said. It's Daddy.

I waited, unsure what to say. These calls always pulled up a mix of emotions—but by now, mostly numbness. I wanted to care more, to feel excited to hear his voice, but I didn't. He was my father, but he was a stranger.

We spoke, our conversation halting and forced. He had heard about my test—how, I wasn't sure—and knew I wouldn't be going to medical school this time around.

After a few minutes of polite conversation, he paused. Silence hung between us.

Finally, he said in Romanian, "Do you want to come visit me in America?"

The silence returned, this time filled with my racing heart and a quick look to my mother, who was now standing by the kitchen sink pretending to dry dishes. She met my eyes and mouthed *ce?*—what? I pursed my lips and took a breath, returning to the conversation with my father.

"I will ask my mother," I finally replied, remembering that, when he had invited me the year before, she had said no.

A few minutes later, we hung up and I told my mom about the call and my father's invitation. To my surprise, she left the decision to me.

"You're eighteen now," she said. I was seventeen last time he called, and now I was an adult. I could make my own choice about whether to visit him in the United States.

That night, as I lay in bed in the dark of my room, staring at the ceiling I couldn't see, I wondered about the trip I already knew I would take. The father I didn't know but wanted so desperately to have a relationship with, not because of who he was but for what he represented: a father with the possibility of becoming a dad. The man who had left a hole in my life that my family and Padre tried hard to fill—but one that, in my mind, could only be filled by my real father. A man I knew so little about, a man who had fled my home country, a man who had nothing and everything to do with who I was and who I would become.

I closed my eyes in an effort to sleep, the thoughts continuing to whirl through my brain like a windstorm. Pulling the quilt up and wriggling to comfort in the bed, I finally accepted my decision.

I wanted to meet my father. I wanted to know the man who had given me half of my DNA. While my family had taken me on a few trips to his home village to meet his family in Globu Craiovei, that was the extent to which I understood my roots. I was interested to know who this man was. And now that I was eighteen, it was my decision.

Yes, I'd go to America. Just for a couple of months. I'd bring my textbooks and keep my studies up so I could successfully retake my medical school exams the following July. I'd experience the United States in all its Western ways and see movies and walk through parks and share meals with my father. Maybe I'd learn why he'd left and why he'd stayed gone. I didn't love him and wasn't sure if I ever would, but curiosity drove me to want to visit him. A desire to understand my father, the other half of my genetics.

I wanted to know him. And maybe through understanding him, I'd understand more about myself.

SECOND LIFE IN AMERICA (DEATH)

"The trauma said, 'Don't write these poems.
Nobody wants to hear you cry about the grief inside your bones.'
[. . .] My bones said, 'Write the poems.'"
—Andrea Gibson, *The Madness Vase*

5

THE PLANE OUT OF COMMUNISM

The New York City sky was gray as we pulled into John F. Kennedy International Airport. As I peered out the window, I grimaced at how ugly the city looked. Gloomy. Not the shiny, glittering America I'd hoped for.

I rubbed my face, my flat palm moving from my right cheek, to my chin, to my left cheek, willing myself to both wake up and calm down at the same time. It had been more than twenty-four hours since I'd left Brăila, traveling by train to București and by taxi to București Otopeni International Airport, where I went through customs. I then flew into Frankfurt, where I had a four-hour layover, and now I was arriving at JFK, where my father would meet me. We would fly together to Boston and drive to his home in Amherst, New Hampshire.

My eyes watered from exhaustion and my body felt achy. Underneath the fatigue, though, was the knowledge that I'd see my father for the first time since I was six years old, that day in my school entryway when I refused his gift of a pen. Now it was 1987 and thirteen years had passed. What would it be like to see him again?

As the Lufthansa plane taxied on the gunmetal-gray runway, I stared up at the silver-gray clouds and thought of all I'd gone through over the past months preparing for this moment. Due to the political climate in Romania, I wasn't able to simply apply for a passport and receive it a few weeks later. Instead, I had to be invited for a visit and submit the invitation letter to the government to get permission to receive a passport. Because of my father's dissident status, it had taken special efforts to be granted a visa to the United States. But since I have extended family in Romania and was actively preparing to go to medical school, they decided there wasn't a strong risk of me staying in America. After receiving my passport, I had to travel by train with my mom to București for an appointment at the American embassy to request a travel visa, enabling me to stay up to two months in the United States of America. Once I had all the approvals and documents, my father bought my roundtrip ticket.

The plane approached the terminal now, and I eyed the looming airport. It was not so different than Romania's airports, at least from the outside. The hulking whitish-gray building fit the color scheme. Gray and white planes taxied in and out of terminals; men in yellow vests drove about in little white trucks. As our plane approached the gate and came to a stop, I noticed a large, empty truck driving our direction, presumably to collect luggage.

My own luggage was in the overhead bin: a small suitcase with a few outfits, my anatomy book, two notebooks with my chemistry and physics reviews, and basic toiletries. I carried only a purse, which had my documents for immigration and, when I'd left, had contained food from my mom for the flight: a sandwich made of cured meat, an apple, some nuts. I'd eaten the food long ago, but while I should have been hungry, my stomach felt something other than hunger.

This emptiness in my gut seemed more metaphorical. I felt as if my insides were being wrung with two hands, twisted in anticipation of meeting my father.

Would I recognize him? Would he recognize me? Would we hug each other? Shake hands? Would we have anything to talk about on the flight to Boston and long drive to Amherst?

The speakers boomed me out of my thoughts with what I recognized as English. I glanced over at my seatmate, who was unbuckling and gathering her things, so I did the same. Opening my purse, I checked again for my passport and documents, which were safely tucked into the side pocket. Suddenly, there was a ding and the plane erupted with movement. In my position toward the back of the plane, I craned my neck to see the people in the front rows retrieving their items from the overhead bins.

When an opening finally cleared for my row, I stood and reached into the overhead bin to pull down my suitcase. By the time I made it to the hallway that led to the terminal entrance, my heart was pounding. Those hands on my gut were wringing harder, faster. Taking a breath, I stepped to the side of the hallway to collect myself. Setting my suitcase down, I used both palms to smooth my curly hair, feeling the wild strands in the back that resulted from hours against an airplane seat. I looked down at the outfit my mother had bought for the trip: a white T-shirt, bright red windbreaker, blue jeans, and white Velcro sneakers. Then I took a breath, picked up my suitcase, and walked deliberately toward the international terminal, where, just beyond customs and immigration, I knew my father would be waiting for me.

As I made my way down the terminal hallway, emotions pulsed through me. I was about to meet my father in person, this stranger of nearly nineteen years. We were linked to one another by genes, nothing more. Would we find any connection beyond the science that bound us?

Despite my lack of English, getting into the country went smoothly, and soon I was walking down the international passageway, where my father would be waiting for me. I searched a multitude of strange faces, all turning their heads this way and that, searching for their own visitors. Scanning the faces one by one, I did not see my father. When I reached the end of the line of people, I turned to search again, my body tense. What if he wasn't there?

I examined the crowd, looking for the man I had only seen photos of in recent years. Does a daughter know her father by sight, even if she hasn't seen him in more than a decade? Does a father know a daughter? Would we recognize each other?

Finally, I saw a man making his way toward me. It must be him, I thought. His family and mine were spot on when they'd told me I look just like him—a comment that used to make me mad but was now a proven fact. We made eye contact and smiled.

As I walked toward him, I took in his appearance. Dark features. Wide shoulders. Fit frame. Short, maybe five-foot-three, and wearing a dark blue fitted business suit, pressed white collared shirt, red tie, and black dress shoes.

Finally, he was standing right in front of me, and I hugged him hello.

I did not feel anything meaningful in that hug. Not love. Not connection. Not familiarity. Not a father-daughter bond. Nothing. Only numbness mixed with uncertainty and a small bit of hope that we could have a somewhat-real relationship by the end of my trip.

We were two people who didn't know each other. Strangers meeting for the first time.

But I was too tired in that moment to analyze my feelings. Nausea sat solidly in my gut, and my limbs ached from the immobility of the long travel and lack of sleep.

"*Fiica mea, bine ai venit!*" my father said. Daughter, welcome!

"*Bună, tată,*" I replied, smiling. Hello, father.

He looked older than I'd expected, which made sense since my most recent photo was probably ten years old. He stood just a little taller than me but wore heeled shoes that gave him extra height. His brown hair was peppered with gray and combed back, revealing a wide forehead, long sideburns, and round eyes slanted slightly downwards toward his ears and framed with thick, bushy eyebrows. He had the "Vrâncuța family nose," with a slight hump at the top of its bridge, hovering over a thick mustache, making him look very serious. And a thick, friendly mutton beard ended at the top of his necktie knot, so wide it hid his neck.

"How was your travel?" he asked in Romanian.

"It was fine," I replied. "But I'm exhausted and ready to sleep."

"Yes, the travel from Romania is long," he said.

I nodded. "Very long."

He picked up my suitcase and motioned in the direction of what I assumed was our next flight. "Shall we?"

I nodded, walking next to him toward the gate for our flight to Boston, weaving between people and talking about my long trip and his travel to meet me. English hummed in the background like loud, indecipherable white noise. The commotion in the airport was almost soothing: television screens mounted on walls, with words I couldn't read streaming across them; people talking loudly to each other; a loudspeaker interrupting every so often to announce something I couldn't understand.

It wasn't long before we had made our short flight to Boston and were in my father's car, driving to his home in New Hampshire. As we rolled slowly through traffic out of Boston, I stared, exhausted, out my window, taking in the dark, overcast sky. High-rises loomed on every side, their bricks wet from rain. Cars crowded the roads and a stream of people crossed streets.

In my tired state, it all looked incredibly dreary and cold—not at all like the light, fun, inviting United States of America I'd envisioned. Where were the sunshine and colors? The car sped up as we exited the city, and all I could think was, *I want to go home.*

We drove for about another hour, mostly in silence. A mix of exhaustion and shyness kept me mostly mute, responding politely to the few attempts at small talk my father made, exchanging surface-level discussion like a taxi driver dropping a passenger at a destination. The emotions I'd expected were still nonexistent. I felt neither happy nor sad. The only strong feeling: home-sickness. At one point, I must have fallen asleep, because the next thing I knew, we were pulling up to an apartment complex.

My mom had told me my father had a nice house in America, and I was curious to see where he lived. I knew he lived alone, having separated from his second wife, who lived in California with their daughter and her daughter from a previous marriage. I had pictured my father living in a two-story home with a manicured lawn and mailbox.

I eyed the apartment building curiously. *This* was the nice house he told my mother he'd bought in America? The mailing address said Amherst, but this apartment was in Milford, a nearby lower-status town. I was confused but too tired and jet-lagged to attempt making sense of the details.

We made our way up a set of stairs to his third-floor apartment. When he opened the door, I noticed a cat greeting us shyly from underneath a desk in the living room. I walked toward the desk and squatted down. The cat was beautiful, a blue-eyed Siamese with pearl fur and a soft gray color on her face, tail, and paws.

"Hi there," I said, *tsk*ing my mouth and holding out my fingers. The cat held camp under the desk but lifted its head at me as if to say hello.

"That's Suzette," my father said. "Come. I'll show you to your room."

Sleep deprivation was starting to hit me, and the next hour or so blurred as I settled into the only bedroom, called my mom to let her know I'd gotten in, and bade my father goodnight as he made his way to the makeshift bed on the living room pullout couch. I fell asleep within minutes, my exhausted brain and body sighing in relief at finally getting to shut down.

—

I woke early the next morning, still on Romanian time, and instantly felt off. My stomach was still sick, my head hurt, and my muscles ached. As I sat up and stretched my arms, my thoughts felt jumbled too, a mix of exhaustion from the travel and not being adjusted to the new time zone.

Great, I thought. *Just what I need on my first real day in America.*

I tried to push my physical discomfort out of my mind as I sifted through my open suitcase on the floor, looking for an outfit to wear that day. Within thirty minutes, I had showered, dressed, made my bed, and put away most of my clothes, which wasn't a big task considering I hadn't brought much. My suitcase was neatly placed in the closet, and I was ready to see the United States and get to know my father.

After breakfast, my father drove us into town to pick up groceries. The American grocery store was rich in food, each aisle bursting with color and options. In Romania, we were still on strict rations, and good produce and meat were hard to find. In America, one could walk up to a meat counter and ask for whatever cut they wanted. Carts overflowed with packaged foods and precut vegetables; bags of lettuce and piles of shrink-wrapped meat; burger buns and blue boxes with pictures of pasta and cheese on the front; big jugs of juice, large bottles of soda, bags of coffee. America seemed to have a limitless supply of foods in pretty packaging.

There was also an exhaustive number of choices for almost every product. In Romania, each product had only one option: a tube of toothpaste, a bar of hand soap, a carton of milk, a bunch of carrots, or a bag of white flour. But in America, it seemed the concept was "the more the better." The volume seemed overwhelming.

For dinner, we selected two lobsters and potatoes to bake as a side. As we went through the checkout line, I wondered what lobster would taste like. After my father paid, we headed back to the apartment to cook together.

Later that night, my father and I sat at the small table in his apartment, plates empty and my heart feeling a little fuller. We were still strangers, but at least our conversation was growing a little more comfortable. The meal was delicious: juicy, flaky lobster and buttery baked potatoes felt exotic and rich after years of simple foods in Romania. But my stomach didn't agree with my tastebuds, as my nausea seemed to grow by the minute. I also still had mental fog, like I was moving in slow motion and not fully present, but at least I had a good first dinner with my father.

An hour later, I vomited violently in the bathroom. I went to bed early, clutching my stomach and shaking, willing chills to subside.

The next morning, I awoke and instantly felt itchy. When I pulled my arms out from under the covers to examine my skin, I noticed small, blister-like bumps extending from the backs of my hands to my shoulders. Standing, I pulled up the leg of my pajamas and saw the same rash on my legs and feet; I opened the top of my pants and saw it on my thighs as well. My hands drifted to my face, where I felt the same bumpy rash on my forehead, cheeks, and neck. The bumps looked almost like chickenpox. I guessed the rash was from stress or a reaction to the change in climate and didn't think much of it.

But looking back, maybe it was my body telling me: Flee, Luissa, get out of here. Run like your life depends on it—because it does.

Of course, I didn't pick up on the message my body was sending me and within a few days the rash had subsided. Instead, I blamed the skin reaction on the lobster and overall stress of the last few days' events.

The rash now gone, I turned my attention to enjoying the first week in America with my father: visiting a natural science museum, walking through a nearby park that had a small dam and lake in it, taking in the green grass and blooming trees of spring. The week also included driving with him to his mailbox in Amherst, the rich part of town, which he kept for appearance's sake; going to Bedford Presbyterian Church in the rich town of Bedford, New Hampshire, on Sunday, where the parking lot was filled with expensive, shiny cars and the chapel with rich, shiny people; shopping in Nashua, a bigger town with better shops; eating our meals together; getting to know each other. We were less strangers now and more acquaintances who held some familiarity—almost a relationship but not quite.

Still, there were signals that caused me to keep a safety bubble around my heart. This man had been absent most of my life. I'd spent nearly nineteen years without a father, and one good week wasn't going to change the fact that he'd deserted me, that he'd broken my mother's heart and showed no remorse. As I got to know him, I also noticed that he moved about the world in a sort of half-truth. He'd told my mother he had a nice home in America; instead, he lived in a cheap, one-bedroom apartment next to the railroad tracks and across from a cemetery. He lived in Milford but drove to Amherst to collect his mail, a ten-minute drive just to claim an address that made him look wealthy. At church the past Sunday, I'd heard him talking with the wealthy parishioners about Peace on Earth, a nonprofit he supposedly ran for Romanian refugees to help them establish a life in the United States. I couldn't be certain, but I didn't think he ran any sort of organization. Plus, he wasn't even Baptist, let alone religious, so why did we go to that church? I guessed it was to build his reputation and appear wealthy.

Then there were his mannerisms. Something about his general disposition didn't feel right to me. While I couldn't put my finger on it, something was off. But what? He'd been nothing but nice to me since I'd arrived, taking me to sightsee and shop. He'd paid for all my meals. He'd made small talk and listened while I told him of my dream to become a doctor.

So what was it? I couldn't pinpoint why, but my unease was undeniably growing.

One evening, during our usual dinner at his apartment, my father said something that broke the carefree mood of the trip and confirmed the internal alarms that had been quietly sounding since I had arrived.

"Now that you're here," he began, his Romanian slow and purposeful. "Let's figure out what we are going to do for you to stay."

"What?" I said, not sure I'd heard him correctly.

"We need to figure out how you'll stay," he repeated.

Where had this come from? I stared at my plate for several seconds, trying to find words to reply.

"I'm not sure I understand," I finally said. "I have no intention of staying."

A long silence followed. I suddenly felt as if I was all alone at the edge of a cliff, with no way to escape this unwanted conversation. In the past, I'd always had my mom—my anchor—to turn to in uncomfortable moments. This was the first time I had faced a confrontation with an adult without my mom to support me. I was all alone.

He frowned, thick eyebrows drawing inward as he stared at me across the table. "What do you think I brought you here for?"

The hair on the back of my neck lifted. I could almost feel the weight of my heart bumping against my ribcage.

"I'm not—"

"I don't have money to waste just for you to visit."

I stared at him, he at me. Moments ago, we'd been enjoying dinner and having a pleasant conversation. It was like he shape-shifted in front of me, but the only thing that changed was his mood. His words, body language, facial expression—they had flipped instantly. While he'd been relaxed and leaning back in his chair moments earlier, now he was leaning forward, elbows on the table, his shoulders drawn toward his ears, staring me down. He looked almost manic. His expression frightened me.

"I don't plan on staying here," I said again. "I don't know what you thought, but it has never been my intention to stay. If I'd known you thought that, I never would have come to begin with."

"Then why did you come here?" he replied, his tone growing sharper.

"To meet you."

"You must have an agenda. Who sent you?"

I stared at him. What was he talking about? Who sent me? He brought me here!

"Who sent you?" he demanded again. His eyes were wide now, his expression drawn tight, dark eyebrows framing his rage.

"No one sent me, Father. You . . . you invited me."

"You must work for the Securitate."

"What? No, I—"

"Who is it? Tell me their name. Who are you working with?"

My body was electric, my heartbeat pulsing to my fear. I felt my body lean away as he crept closer to me from across the table, his hands now heavy on the surface, his face growing red, his eyes vacillating from squinting at me, studying me, to growing wide with anger. I ached to leave, to run all the way back to Romania. If only I had wings, I would have flown away.

"Father, where is this coming from?"

"Who is it?" he repeated. "Tell me! Who sent you?"

What the hell is going on here? I thought.

This was coming from nowhere. Everything was fine just moments ago. But looking at his enraged face, I knew there was no getting through to him that night. I wanted to go home. I wanted my mom, my grandma, my grandpa. I wanted to be back in Romania, where I was safe and loved and not in this tiny apartment with this man who was terrifying me.

"I need to go to bed," I finally said, standing. He said nothing, but I felt his gaze on my back the entire walk to the bedroom. Once inside, I shut the door, leaned my back against the wood, and slid to the floor, trying to make sense of what had just happened. My rational brain couldn't piece together the puzzle of my father. It was like two people lived inside his body. Or maybe it was one person who was very good at acting. Either way, I had seen enough. I knew then that my father would never have my love.

Still, even with this realization, I had no idea what to do. I'd never dealt with anger like his. I'd grown up in a cocoon, surrounded by love and support. The belle of my family, my church, and our relatives, friends, and acquaintances. I could remember my mom raising her voice at me just a couple of times, and only when I really deserved it. No one had ever looked at me like that, accused me like that; and I didn't know what to do.

My heart was still racing. Fight or flight—I'd learned about that in school. My brain wanted me to run. To get far away from here. I placated myself with the knowledge that I had my passport and a ticket home. Maybe I could even change my flights to leave early. Should I call my mom the next day and see if we could?

That night, after dressing for sleep, I lay on the cool fabric of my pillow and stared at the moonlight that drew a line across my wall. My thoughts drifted to dinner and my father's horrible expression and the chill I'd felt when he looked at me. I took a breath, closed my eyes, and thought of my family and how happy I'd be to see them.

Just a few more weeks and I'll be back in Romania, I thought. I can make it a few more weeks. I'll celebrate my birthday in the United States and go home soon after. Once there, I'll hang out with Paul and study for my medical school entrance exams and go to the opera with my mom. It will be like this trip never happened, like a blip in the long story of my life, a short detour in my path to become a doctor, to make my family proud, to be successful and give back to my mother and grandparents because they'd given up so much for me.

Yes, just a few more weeks, I told myself, lying in the dark of my room. Just a few more weeks before I'd be back in Romania, back on the path to the life I'd always planned for myself.

—

After the initial shock of our conversation, I had steeled myself for the next weeks in America. I hoped my father would accept my "no," but instead he kept bringing up me staying. Each time, I replied with the same answer: "No. I am going home to Romania."

Tension grew each day in the apartment. From the moment I woke each morning, I felt like I was walking on melting ice, trying not to break it. Just be careful, I told myself, remembering a Romanian saying: Luissa, *nu da cu mucii în fasole*, don't throw buggers in the beans—don't spoil everything.

Each Sunday, I'd call my mom and talk with her for a few minutes. Hearing her voice reassured me: I would be going home soon.

"*Da, totul este bine, Mami,*" I'd say, not wanting to worry her. Everything is good, Mom.

While I was struggling inwardly, externally I continued on as if everything was normal. My father and I visited historic sites and parks, attended church, barbequed at a park near his apartment. We went on like this, in a forced bubble of normalcy, passing the days playing father and daughter. But in the back of my mind all I wanted was to be back in Romania with my real parents: my mom and grandparents.

And then my nineteenth birthday arrived. I woke early and instantly missed my family. I'd never spent a birthday away from them. We'd always celebrated together: Mom, Grandpa, Grandma, Aunt Tutti, Uncle Sandu, and Dragoș. The women made a multi-course meal and we enjoyed a feast together as a family. I smiled as they brought out *prajitura Boema*, a traditional Romanian layered chocolate birthday cake, singing to me in their sweet voices.

La mulți ani,

cu sănătate,

să vă dea Domnul tot ce doriți.

Zile senine

și fericire

la mulți ani, să trăiți.

Happy birthday,

in good health,

may God grant all your wishes.

Clear days

and happiness

happy birthday to you.

I smiled as I got out of bed and dressed, encouraged by the beautiful days ahead in Romania. Today would be a good day, even if I wasn't where I wanted to be or with the people I wanted to be with.

That day, my father and I ran a couple of errands, including gathering food for our meal later that night. We set the table with a tablecloth and candles. We had dinner, with some red wine, of which I only had a few sips. After the meal, he brought out a store-bought white birthday cake with nineteen candles. I made my secret wish and blew out the candles. He gave me a gold necklace with a cross.

The rest of the night happened as though in Polaroid snapshots.

I remember seeing the wine bottle on the table as my father lowered me onto the cold beige linoleum floor. I remember asking him, "What are you doing?" I remember seeing a strange smile on his face as waves of electric shocks rippled from my brain throughout my whole being. I remember him coming on top of me, his body pinning me under as I asked over and over, "What are you doing?" I remember separating from my body, as if I were no longer a whole self but instead floating beyond the room, beyond my own body, beyond a reality that didn't exist anymore.

I remember the sharp, tearing pain within. And then, darkness.

That is when my father stole everything from me. That is the moment I died.

6

ERASED IDENTITY

In 1984, just a few years before my trip to America, a case study was presented at a meeting of the American College of Neuropsychology. The subject of their research: learned helplessness.

In what would be a banned study today, researchers administered electric shocks to dogs in cages. These weren't little zaps—the dogs were administered painful shocks. Since the animals had nowhere to go because they were locked in cages, they couldn't escape and were forced to endure the pain. Researchers referred to the canines' experience as "inescapable shock." Just thinking of those animals makes my heart ache.

As cruel as this experiment was, what researchers discovered next was profound. The findings shocked the neuropsychological community. After administering the electric shocks, researchers opened the cages and shocked the dogs again. One would expect the dogs to instantly run away. But they didn't try to leave. Instead, they just laid in their torturous cages, with the doors wide open, and whimpered, soiling their cages. They had become so broken that the possibility of freedom—the open door, right in front of them—wasn't psychologically available to them.

When they repeated the open door experiment on another set of dogs that had never been shocked, they immediately bolted out of the cage and ran away.[6]

The night of my birthday, I became like a helpless dog in a cage. I lay in the dark trying to process what had happened. Nothing would compute. It made no sense. It was like I'd been given an electric shock at a voltage so high, in an environment with no clear way to escape, that I broke. Nothing in my young life had prepared me for that day; nothing within me knew how to reconcile my dearest dreams with this nightmare.

I don't know how long I lay there that night before I gathered enough energy to drag myself to my bedroom and sink into my bed. I must have fallen asleep, because the next morning I awoke to sunshine streaming through the edges of my curtains. I lay in my bed for a long while, willing myself to get up. I had to confront what happened.

I had to make sense of it somehow. I had to understand.

I walked to the bathroom. As if in slow motion, I undressed, got into the shower, and turned on the water. Then I stood there, water hitting my body, passively allowing the shower to do its magic and wash it all away: my mind, my body, my soul, my birthday, the memory. Shivers and heat waves alternated within me, so I kept turning the water from hot to cold, hot to cold. Again and again. Finally, I shut off the water and began drying my hair, face, and body with slow, calculated motions. I wanted to feel clean. I didn't.

I brushed my hair, allowing it to air dry. Dressing slowly and deliberately, I ran what I would say to him over and over in my mind. I anticipated his explanations and thought of my responses. My stomach felt hollow; my soul empty. It was as if a brush fire had risen unexpectedly out of nowhere and swept over me, leaving desolation in its wake.

At nineteen, I was technically an adult. I felt I should know how to handle this situation—to take care of myself and not burden my family. But in truth, I was naïve to the world in so many ways. I'd had one kiss with one boy—and then asked him not to kiss me again because I was worried I could get pregnant. I'd had no sexual education. I had no real experience of

---

6 Bessel A. van der Kolk, M.D., *The Body Keeps the Score*, 2nd ed. (New York, Penguin Books: 2015) 29–30.

a father-daughter relationship. I knew what he'd done to me was vile, but I also had no one to turn to and nowhere to go, and although I knew I'd done nothing wrong, shame festered within me.

I wanted to crawl into a dark quiet corner, lay there in the fetal position, and allow myself to grieve, process, heal, and plan. Something within me had shattered. Would I be able to put myself back together? Maybe. Maybe not. Would my life ever look the same? It couldn't. Not to me.

My family . . . I couldn't imagine what it would do to them if they found out. I wanted nothing more than to call my mom, to tell her everything, to cry into the phone and beg her to buy me a ticket that day. But I knew I could never do that.

My family could never know. Never.

No, this was my burden to bear, and I'd do anything to wash away this trauma, reorient my life, and achieve my dream of becoming a doctor.

When I came into the main room of the apartment that morning, I saw my father sitting at the kitchen table. He had a newspaper and a coffee like it was any morning. Like my whole life had not just been destroyed the night before. Like he'd done nothing wicked, nothing disgraceful. Like he was just a normal father on a normal morning with his normal coffee and paper.

He kept his eyes on the paper and didn't acknowledge my presence.

My gut twisted again. I felt like I was going to throw up.

"We need to talk," I said.

He set down his paper and looked at me but said nothing.

"What happened last night?" I began. "I don't understand what happened. I want to talk about it."

He studied me but remained silent. I couldn't read his expression: slightly narrowed eyes, drawn mouth.

Why wasn't he speaking? Was this a game to him? Had he intended for that night all along?

"I just want to go home," I went on, my voice deepening as I held in tears. "I was never meant to come here. I didn't want to come here." Emotion choked in my throat, a mix of fear and pain. But I would not cry in front of this man.

He angled his seat to face me, the chair legs making a loud scraping sound that echoed through my bones.

"What can I do?" he said. "How can I get you to stay?"

I breathed in sharply and my skin prickled. I suddenly felt lightheaded. As I stood there, looking at the stranger before me, tingling fear swept across my scalp, my shoulders, my gut, my legs.

"I will never stay here. I want to go home."

"You have another month," he said. "Then you can go."

His words sounded tinny, like I was listening through a wall, detached from my own body. He was the only one who could change my ticket to go home early, and it was clear there was no way he would do that. I would have another four weeks in this hellish apartment with this evil man. I felt like I could be sick right there on the floor.

"The only reason I came was to see my father," I said. "To get to know you. This is not what I deserve. This is not what I want. I want to go home."

He studied me for what felt like minutes. Then, picking up his paper, he said, "I'd like you to stay."

I wanted nothing more than to leave. To run far away, to escape back to Romania where I was safe and loved and had my family, Padre, and my boyfriend waiting for me. I had come to America full of cautious hope . . . and here I was, with hope replaced by a pain I wasn't sure would ever leave my body.

Yes, I could run out of the apartment. But where would I go?

Yes, I could tell someone, but who? I didn't know anyone in America. And how? I didn't speak English or know how the legal system worked in this foreign country. And if I did succeed and my father was arrested, where would that leave me? On the street?

Yes, I could try to go to the airport and get a ticket home, but how would I get there? And if I made it, with what money would I buy a ticket?

Yes, I could ask for help from my family. But what would I say? I didn't want them to know anything was wrong. I couldn't burden them with this shame. And anyway, what could they do all the way from Romania, especially when they didn't speak English or understand the American system either?

I was a young woman with no life-survival skills in a foreign country. I had no language, no money, no status, no one to turn to, no hope, and no future. In this country of possibilities, I was a nobody. A lost person in a strange place. If I ran away, I would become another sad statistic in this "land of milk and honey," as we foreigners see America.

Without a support system, language, or citizenship, my father held the keys to my locked cage. And he would keep shocking me until the open door wasn't psychologically available to me anymore.

And he did.

—

Three weeks later, my locked cage would gain another padlock as I sat in a government office in Boston, watching the immigration officer talk with my father in English. Next to the paperwork that bore my name was a long affidavit my father had written on my behalf, in English, detailing why I should receive political asylum in America. At the top was that day's date: June 8, 1987. At the bottom was my name, which I'd carefully signed in front of the officer, my father standing just behind my right shoulder, making sure I went through with his plan.

As the still-foreign sound of English faded into the background of my awareness, I thought of the previous weeks with my father. I felt like I was floating through my own life in a half-detached state, trying to make sense of the situation I'd found myself in.

Less than two months earlier, I'd been in Romania with my loving family. I had my studies and Paul and friends and church. Padre. Bîzu. Sandu, Tutti, Dragoş. I was vibrant and innocent and hopeful about the future. Loved. Protected.

Now, in the stale immigration office, I knew I could never return to that life. While I couldn't decipher the contents of the affidavit, I knew my father had written a detailed account of why I couldn't return to my country: that I'd been persecuted in Romania because of his political dissident status. That I hadn't been allowed to see him. That going back would be dangerous. That I would be interrogated by the Securitate about his political aspirations and anticommunist writings, speeches, and propaganda as a political dissident in free America. And that my failure to cooperate with the Securitate would put my life and that of my family in jeopardy.

None of this was true. While there were hardships in communism, I never felt threatened or worried for my safety. My family had good standing in the community, and my mother and uncle were connected in the upper political echelons. I had opportunity before me, including attending medical school. But now that those words had been written and filed with the United States, with my signature at the bottom, there was no going back. Not to Romania, not to my old life. I was now an enemy of the state.

I looked at the man behind the desk holding the key to my American future. He was middle-aged, prematurely balding, and clean shaven, with a pointy nose and thin lips that held a slight upward tilt in the corners, giving him a perpetual smile. He wore black-rimmed glasses that reminded me of my high school Romanian literature professor, Mr. Ungur, but with a kinder face. I saw him glance toward me and then say something to my father. He pointed to the form, spoke, and then gestured for my father to translate.

"He says he will file your affidavit and we'll hear back in a couple of weeks," my father said. After a pause, he added: "You will surrender your Romanian passport as well."

I nodded quietly, wishing I could reach across the desk, grab the letter, and rip it to shreds. I wanted to scream at the man behind the desk: "I don't want this! I don't want this!" I was the dog in the cage.

But with the signed affidavit and the loss of my Romanian identity, I had already sealed my fate. So instead, I asked my father, "How long until I can become a citizen?"

"Three years."

I nodded again and looked down at my lap, processing another three years with my father. At least my mother would be coming soon. He'd promised. It was one of the conditions of me staying. I couldn't imagine a life without her. She was my world.

As their conversation continued, I thought of the conversation my father and I had had days earlier. He'd asked what it would take to get me to stay.

I'd said nothing in the world could convince me to stay with him. I wanted to go home to Romania, to leave him forever and never return. I wanted to be with my mom.

And then he said something that, in my broken state, sounded like a lifeline: "What if I promise to bring your mother here? What if I remarry her and help you go to medical school?"

His words were strategic. He knew my greatest dream in life was to become a doctor. He knew my mother was the most important person in my entire world, that she was the sun that rose and set in my life.

When he made that promise, a tiny bud of hope bloomed in my chest, taking root in my shame. If my mom came, if my family got back together, maybe things would be normal again. Maybe I could wash away the outrage and disgust I felt toward my father. It was almost like I could turn back time and undo what happened on my birthday. I could have a father again.

All I wanted was to be normal. All I wanted was a whole family—and a father who loved me and cared for me the way a father should.

I would never have stayed just to go to medical school. That was too much of a price to pay. But if I could have both school and my mom, and a chance at normalcy . . .

The idea of normal was powerful.

If I stayed under the conditions he offered, I reasoned, maybe I could eventually have a normal life. I'd be able to pursue my career, learn English, be independent. Become a physician and achieve my dream. Be with my mom. My mind spun a fairytale—something to hang on to as I struggled not to fall off an emotional and psychological cliff.

Over the years, I have reprocessed my thoughts, reasonings, and actions from those initial horrific days. Neuroscience tells us that childhood experiences affect our behaviors and personality into adulthood even if we were not aware of the existence of this connection. Moreover, the immature, traumatized young brain creates intensely convoluted and highly fictitious modalities to shield from self-destruction.

Of course, I did not know about behavioral neuroscience at that time, so I came up with my own explanation: "It all comes full circle, be it good or bad."

My whole self was grasping at straws. Anything and everything to keep from drowning. I repeated to myself: "My screw-up. It's my job to clean it up."

I had my own iron-clad assessment, one that kept me ashamed and trapped. It went like this: It was all my fault that I decided to make this trip, that I believed in this man whom I called "Father," that I believed I could get to know him well enough for him to become a "dad" after all, that I believed deep inside he could become part of a now-whole family. How could I be so gullible?

But it didn't really matter. I was there now. With no do-over. My mess. My job to clean it up.

Then, at my darkest moment, he promised to remarry my mother and help me become a doctor. My two dreams for one seemingly small price, to remain here in America. I wondered why he was doing this and decided it had to be out of remorse. Maybe he wanted to make things right for my mom, for us. He said he wanted me to become a doctor too.

I told myself: This will solve everything. I will fix my wrong. I will deal with my pain, shame, and scars. No one will know.

I will keep my wounds covered until I am ready to tend to them. Surely I can do it.

So I took another leap of faith, and I believed. Again.

That day, when he made his padlock offer, I trusted him.

"When will that happen?" I asked him.

"As soon as we sign the paperwork."

"Right after?"

He nodded. "We'll do that, and then you're going to start school."

I considered his words. Not knowing anything about medical school in America, I assumed it must be easier to be admitted than in Romania if I could start right away. He'd been here since 1976, had attended college in the United States, and even worked as a professor at New Hampshire Vocational Technical College. He must know how it all works, I told myself. The language barrier would be a challenge, but if I started with calculus or physics, maybe I could get by. The alphabets were similar, and science has so many Latinate words.

Plus it was only May. School started in September, so I'd have time to learn some English.

"As soon as it's done?"

"Yes."

"She must never know what happened," I said. "You can never tell her. It will kill her."

He nodded again. "First we do the paperwork."

Now, sitting at the immigration desk, I felt that familiar nausea creep into my gut. I thought of my grandparents. If my mom was the sun, they were the moon. The other light in my universe.

Before I had left Romania, one of my greatest joys was surprising my grandma with breakfast. After she had her gallbladder taken out, she was on a special diet that she wasn't too keen on following. While I couldn't cook much, I did know how to make a simple breakfast with soft boiled eggs, freshly homemade ricotta cheese, and Turkish coffee. Seeing her smile when she saw her dear grandchild serving her each morning—well, that was the best payment I could ever receive. I thought of my grandfather, whose greatest hope for me was to have a better life, to reach my dreams. I hoped my decision to stay in America and attend medical school here would bring him pride and not pain.

We left that day and drove back to Milford in silence. I stared out the window, watching the trees and cars swish by in the passenger rearview mirror, thinking of my life fading into the distance with them.

I had signed my life away that morning. I had no country, no language, no family close by. I had even surrendered my true full name during the day's proceedings, at my father's insistence—he had changed his own surname since I had been born and now wanted mine to be the same. It felt like a claim of ownership, which I despised.

It was like my old self had died and my new self was born again in America—nineteen years old, alone, and new to this broken world I had never wanted.

That Sunday, I called my mom like usual. My voice was low, my words few.

"I'm not coming home," I told her, struggling not to cry into the receiver. "I've decided to stay." Her gasp and silence were all the response I needed to know that I'd broken her heart.

I had tried to make my voice sound positive, like I had been given an opportunity, but I knew I hadn't done a good job hiding my sadness. Her silence continued and I wasn't sure if she would ever recover from the shock. Could she feel my pain from across the ocean?

Just then, my father ripped the phone away from my ear and started shouting at her. "Do you understand? She is not coming back. Leave her the hell alone!" Then he slammed the phone into its cradle, the sound reverberating through my thoughts.

What had happened? I was confused at his outburst, my nervous system electric with emotional pain and physical distress. My eyes swam with tears but I blinked them away. I would not cry in front of this monster. Not now. Not ever.

—

About a week later, I sat across the table from my father, poking at the chicken and potatoes I'd attempted to make for dinner. The ache of the afternoon distracted me and I had no appetite. My father had gotten a call from the immigration office that day, notifying him that they were changing my permanent residency application paperwork from political asylum to immigrant. He'd told my father it was better to go the immigrant route, even though it meant an additional two years until I could apply for citizenship, with a total of five years. I couldn't fully understand the reasoning behind this change, but I guessed there were less political implications for the two governments and less paperwork for the immigration officer. Nobody knew about my saga, so what would an extra two years matter to them? To add insult to injury, my five-year clock hadn't even begun ticking—I still had to wait for my green card.

As difficult as this news was, what could I do? I felt trapped. The minute I applied for political asylum, when I signed my name to that litany of lies my father wrote, I became an enemy of the state. I no longer had a passport or any other identification until I got my green card. There was no going back to Romania.

Plus, I had already told my mom about my decision. Shortly after she delivered the news to my grandparents, my grandma had to be admitted to the mental health unit Cobăleanu in Brăila for a profound nervous breakdown, and my grandpa was admitted in the hospital with acute inflammation of the pancreas and liver from the emotional stress. Adding to the stress of my grandparents' ill health, my mother had the stress of her own broken heart.

Thankfully, though, her heart wouldn't be broken for long. My father had promised to bring her to America soon.

I took a small bite of potato and glanced at my father, who was hunched over his plate and eating quickly. The only conversation was between the dishes: his fork clanking on the plate; knife grinding as he cut meat.

Finally, I asked, "When will my mother come?"

He set down his fork and chewed slowly before answering. "What do you mean?"

"What do you mean, 'what do I mean'?" I shot back.

When he picked up his glass to drink, I went on. Words spilled out of me like the water from an overturned glass.

"First, you lied to me, you humiliated me on my birthday—you raped me and took my virginity. Me, your very flesh and blood." I took a deep breath in, pushing the memory from my thoughts. "Then, you said to me—you promised me—that you are going to bring my mom here. You made me stay here. You wrote the letter to apply for political asylum. You wrote all that stuff about how they didn't allow me to see you and that it's unsafe for me there when in reality you are the one who didn't care to have anything to do with me all my life. Now I'm an enemy of the state. I cannot go home."

I paused, my face hot and eyes stinging. I blinked quickly and tightened my jaw as I added, "You have to do what you promised. You have to bring her here so we can be"—hot tears were forming at the corners of my eyes now, and I swallowed quickly to keep my emotions inside—"so we can be a family."

My father's eyes squinted into little slits. He set his glass down, pushed his plate away, and folded his hands in front of him, angling his body toward me.

I leaned back instinctively and held my breath. My heart raced as I forced myself to exhale and steel my expression so he wouldn't see my fear.

He finally spoke, drawing his words out slowly. "As long as I live, your mother will never come here."

The words echoed inside my brain, bouncing off my skull, like a leopard pacing in a cage, hitting the walls, hoping to find a crack, a flaw, an opening. There was none.

That was the moment I realized my mistake. My huge, irrevocable, life-changing mistake. I had trusted this horrid man with my future—my life. I had wanted "normal" so badly that I'd given up everything I knew, everything I loved.

I stared back at him, saying nothing. He won't break me, I told myself. He won't. I still have medical school. I still have my dream.

Even then, even after he'd broken his first promise, I believed his other lie, that he would put me into school to become a doctor in America.

I believed him.

How could I have believed him?

Looking back, I now know the trauma had formed a cloud over my rational thinking. I needed to believe his last promise was true to survive.

I'd been stripped of my identity, my language, and my family. Now I was forced to start my life over. It was like I'd been born again, except it felt like death.

7

BROKEN WINGS CAN'T FLY

I rubbed my hand over my bald head, my palm running over the prickled surface, fingers falling along the back of my scalp as I studied myself in the mirror. My face was gaunt. I touched my cheek: running from jawline to chin, down my neck, across my chest, resting the flat of my palm over my heart.

Turning on the water, I let it run, testing the temperature with my index finger every few seconds. When it felt cold, I cupped the water and washed my face, then placed my now cold fingers on the back of my neck. This "crisp" feeling always startled me and helped me snap out of the numbness and feeling of hopelessness; washing my skin temporarily rinsed away shame and pain. After years of this prison, years with my father, these little rituals kept me sane.

As I picked up the towel off the rack and dried my face slowly, I remembered the baths I took as a young child, and my mother's loving expression as she held up a towel for me, wrapping me in its softness, then helping me dry and dress. I would give anything for that moment—for a minute of innocence. Freedom.

My hand drifted to my scalp again as I thought of how my mother used to brush my hair each morning. How she'd bring half of my thick curls up into a ponytail, letting the rest flow over my shoulders, and tie them in colorful ribbons to match my outfits. How she carefully cut my hair when I occasionally needed a trim.

I cherished my beautiful curly hair. I never wanted to straighten my curls or hide them. Every time I finally accepted that I needed a trim, my mom was the only one entrusted with this sacred task. I would say to her, "Mami, I need a haircut, but just a little cut, OK?" My poor mother would do as I asked and carefully cut the ends off. Afterward, I would see my curls on the floor and start bawling.

"Why did you cut all my curls?" I'd ask between sobs. "Now I have no more curls!"

And every time, Mom would patiently explain to me that, once I washed my hair, the ends would curl up again, and my hair would be as beautiful as before. I would rush to wash my curls, and even though she was right, it felt like I lost a part of me when those ends were severed.

Now, looking at myself in the mirror, accepting what I had done to myself, I knew shaving my head was another attempt to salvage a dying part of me.

I ran my hand over my head again and the thoughts came sharply. How Mom used to kiss the top of my head while I completed my studies. How she smiled at me across the dinner table each night. How we held hands while walking the promenade and whispered in the theatre and talked of my future as a doctor. She had always been my greatest supporter, my whole strength, my world.

Now I was alone. Broken beyond repair. I kept our love wrapped up, hidden deep inside my being, and only felt its warmth from a distance. I did not feel worthy of anything more, not wanting to spoil a love so happy, so clean. Unsure if I would ever be normal again, deserving of love again.

It was 1992. It had been five years since the birthday that broke me. Five years since I'd agreed to stay in America in my quest for normal—a shattered effort to fix what my father had destroyed within me. Five years of unkept promises, of pain, of fighting for my dreams and my sanity; of being the dog in the cage.

In the early days, weeks, and months with my father, I felt hopeless. After all, I didn't have the tools to navigate chronic, hostile abuse, and being constantly in survival mode, both physically and mentally. But over time, I learned to live with the reality that there was no one in America who would have my back. No one to lean on. No shoulder to cry on.

Within just a few months, I learned to adapt. Sink or swim became my constant reality. I had coped with the loss of my old life, the state of my new life, and the hope that, one day, I would be freed of my torment. In my darkest moments, I clung to this hope.

I returned my gaze to the mirror, holding my own stare, absorbing my features before me. My eyes held the gaunt gray rings of trauma, my cheeks sunken from suffering. My hair gone from the stress; it had started falling out in clumps months earlier. I lost handfuls of curls when washing or brushing, so I'd taken a razor to my scalp one afternoon, finishing the job. I repeated this process a few times over the next couple of weeks because I had read somewhere that doing so would cause the hair to grow back thicker, fuller. But while the loss of my curls only deepened my despair, the hope of something good coming out of my sacrifice gave me the courage to go on.

Who was this woman before me? A shell of Luissa, a broken version of the bright, dynamic young woman I used to be. "Quicksilver," as my uncle would call me. Now I was far from normal. Far from my family. Far from myself.

Making my way toward my bedroom, I willed my limbs to move. Each movement brought a memory.

Walking toward the bedroom . . . the fight to pursue my goal, with my father allowing just one class a semester. My dream was a flickering light going out, slowly fading into a memory.

Opening the bedroom door . . . the three abortions I'd suffered through, sitting in sterile medical offices for the dilation and curettage as the doctor saved my future. As I walked into the bedroom to ready myself for the day, I stood there for several seconds, overcome by the memory of the first abortion: How when it was all done, I had passed out on the bathroom floor of the clinic. How I was still lying there when I woke up to the sound of the nurse knocking on the door and asking, "Are you OK in there?" I mustered a "yes" and dragged myself up, white as a sheet. When she entered the room, she knew I wasn't OK when she saw blood trickling down my legs from under the faded medical gown.

How she had me lay down until I was well enough to leave. How he was waiting at the curbside in the blue Oldsmobile Cutlass S with the license plate "Peace 1," and how the irony had struck me hard that day.

I opened the door that afternoon, got in, and lay down on the back seat, my face turned toward the backrest. Tears flowing quietly, I felt the deepest hollow reigning my soul. I thought: Is this how my first pregnancy is meant to be? Just like all girls, I had dreamed of falling in love with Prince Charming. Of having a beautiful white wedding and sharing the news of being pregnant with a husband I loved. Being happy, proud to share my happiness with the people I love and with the world. Experiencing the arrival of my baby: a new life, a new being.

The subsequent two times found me blunted, incapable of mustering any emotion. My brain was shielding itself from allowing repeated trauma to inflict further damage. The walls were rising tall around me.

Taking off my nightclothes . . . the times I had done so at his will, quietly retreating to the shower afterwards, then burying myself in my bed, with Suzette at my side, my only living friend.

Dressing for the day . . . his reigning paranoia—setting traps around the apartment for "the communists": honey on the doorknob for fingerprints; a thin layer of sawdust on the floor for footprints; audio recording devices when we went out, which he would later listen to intently for hours for any signs of political intruders. He checked on me too, tracking my mileage on the car, recording my phone conversations, and reviewing the bank statements each month and questioning me if anything looked off.

Making my bed . . . the financial lockdown, with just $1 allowance per week, even though I worked at two local grocery stores and for my father's real estate company. My father had each paycheck deposited directly into his accounts, cutting off my access. I could only make deposits, not write checks or take out cash on my own.

Tidying my room . . . the duties I was required to keep up around the house: grocery shopping, cooking, cleaning, managing household finances under his ever-scrutinizing eye. As I straightened and folded, I thought of the apartment that was my prison. We lived on the third floor—the top level so no one could climb in through the window or down from an apartment above to spy on us. The apartment's isolated location was one of the many ways my father separated us from the outside world.

Dressed and with the room made now, I stood in the morning light. It was still early, just seven-thirty in the morning. It would not do any good to focus on what is, I told myself. What is—that is pain. What can be, well—that's worth facing the day before me and continuing on, one step before the other, with the hope that I might somehow achieve what meant so much to me.

I made my way through the apartment, thinking about my chores that day. As I walked past the kitchen, I saw my father still in his makeshift bed. He would be up after eight-thirty, then go for a run and start working at the business at ten.

Reaching the living room, Suzette picked her head up from the chair she was lying on.

"Hey there, girl," I said softly in Romanian. "How's my good girl?"

She jumped up and trotted toward me, stopping short to look up at me with her intelligent blue eyes.

I smiled, bending to run my hand over her head and down her spine as she lifted her bottom and tail and instantly began to purr. I picked her up and held her against me, propping her up like a baby, carrying her to the window overlooking the apartment parking lot.

In the years with my father, Suzette had become my best friend. Petting her head, I smiled at the thought of our afternoon greetings. Every time I came home from school or work, I would pat my left shoulder and she would jump straight up, careful not to claw me as she landed. Then I would reach up, lift her off my shoulder, and hold her, my littlest best friend, a source of strength and comfort.

She was playful too. Every time I'd get back from running along the train tracks behind the apartment, we would play fight, her batting at my covered arm with her soft paws, me batting back. Eventually she'd get tired of playing, fluff up her fur, and hiss—my cue to back off. Suzette was my only real source of love, play, and fun.

Sometimes, when all my chores, work, and homework were done, we would go to the cemetery. I'd carry her across the parking lot and train tracks, setting her down once we reached the paved path between the graves. She'd trot beside me as I walked the grounds or sit next to me as I reclined under one of the many broad trees.

Each night, she tried to nuzzle my head while I slept, purring and rubbing against my face. But in Romania, I was taught to never let an animal near my face while sleeping, so I'd gently push her toward my feet, where she'd cuddle up and sleep all night. She was my calm; my only friend.

"It's a new day, Suzette," I finally said, forcing a lightness in my voice. "I have a lot to do today: work in a couple of hours, class this afternoon. I'm finally taking calculus . . . it's so easy—multiple choice tests!" I had aced calculus my last year of high school, so retaking it in college felt like an easy win.

I stroked her head, thinking through my day. I'd been saving my allowance for a few weeks so I could get a sub sandwich at D'Angelo's before going to school. I could almost taste my favorite—the number nine, a grilled steak sandwich with onions, peppers, mushrooms, and American cheese—and almost feel the simple joy of watching the sandwich maker place the ingredients. I would sit alone at a window table that afternoon, relishing every bite, the flavors dancing in my mouth and my body relaxing in the knowledge that I was safe for the five minutes it took to eat my sandwich. I felt powerful enjoying a meal that I'd saved for and bought for myself. My father didn't know about my secret meals, and I was careful only to go in between activities I was allowed to do like work and school. Plus, it was within walking distance of Shaw's, one of the grocery stores I worked at, so he couldn't question me on the mileage.

"Tomorrow, girl, we'll go for a walk, OK?"

Suzette lifted her chin at me, eyes half-closed, her purr resonating through my entire being.

"I know, I know. I'd like to go today too. But there is no time." I scratched her left ear. She lifted her chin to lean into my hand, and I stroked her chin and neck, smoothing the downy fur with my fingers.

I gently set her down. "Time to work. I have a lot to do before I leave."

Suzette followed me as I walked to the kitchen, staying close at my heels. I washed my hands then gathered flour, yeast, water, and salt. Before I left for work, I needed to bake bread, iron my father's clothes, and pay bills. If I had time, I'd clean the bathroom.

When I came out of the kitchen, my father had left for his run. It was always better when he was gone. I could almost pretend I was a single twenty-something, living in her apartment alone, doing housework for herself, pursuing her dream. No one holding her down or back. No one making her suffer. No one controlling her, forcing her, trying hard to keep her broken.

By the time I'd finished my chores, Suzette had tired of following me around the house and was back in her favorite spot in the living room, cozied up in the chair by my desk. The late morning sun had made its way to her, bathing her pearl fur in sunlight, glistening on her whiskers. I gave her a soft pat on the head, grabbed the keys, and walked out the door and into my day.

—

Back in Romania, communism had fallen a few years earlier, starting with the fall of the Berlin Wall on November 9, 1989. The German people inspired the world with their courage: They pushed back against their government to reunite East and West Germany. Soon, Romanians flooded the streets in protest against their own government, especially in Timișoara, where protestors gathered against Nicolae Ceaușescu. They were tired of living scared. Along with ongoing food, electricity, and gas rations, the Securitate had grown even stronger since I'd left, creating a culture of fear within the country and distrust between neighbors and with the government. People worried for their lives and livelihood and, even if they followed all the rules, struggled under the harsh rations and restrictions.

By late December, the rioting had grown so strong that Ceaușescu and his wife tried to flee by helicopter. When the pilot landed, saying he'd run out of fuel, their bodyguards abandoned them and the two fled by car. Eventually, they were apprehended. A few days later, the news came out that they had been executed by firing squad.[7]

This marked a sea change in Romania. Communism was over.

The news made me thrilled for my family—no longer were they under communist rule; they wouldn't have to suffer from the rations, rules, and fears. But as the Iron Curtain fell and reunited Germany with itself and the rest of Europe, and inspired people in other nations to free themselves from the grips of communism, I knew reuniting with my family was not so simple.

Everything within me wanted to return home, and now I could. There were no political reasons keeping me out, no international borders in my way. I could, at any time, call home to ask for a plane ticket. I could leave my father, give up my pathway to American citizenship and American medical school, and return to Romania, to the love and support of my cocoon. Maybe I could even still build a chrysalis and become a butterfly.

But I knew I couldn't do that. I was too deep in the world I'd unwillingly built in America; too mired in the trauma I'd undergone, too disconnected from the self I'd lost on my nineteenth birthday and many times since. If I went back to Romania, I'd carry with me the shame of what was happening to me. In a way, it would be admitting the trauma I lived everyday with my father was real. If I left, I would never have the "normal" I so desired. I would be forever broken, never mended. If I left, I might miss my chance at realizing my dream—a reality I felt I was making progress toward, even though I was only taking a couple of classes at a time. If I left, what would all this suffering mean? What would have been the point?

No, I was too deep into this life I hadn't chosen. Too broken. Too far from normal to return to the normalcy of my family.

Then there was the damage I'd already done back home. I knew that, shortly after I left, my grandmother had been taken to a psychiatric ward because she was so distraught at losing her granddaughter, and my grandfather

---

7   For more information, see: John Simpson, "How crowds toppled communism's house of cards in 1989," BBC News, December 29, 2019, https://www.bbc.com/news/world-europe-50821545

had become gravely ill. I knew I'd been lying to my mom, in a way, during our Sunday phone calls, asking her for recipes and pretending I was OK. I was not OK. It only took one glance at my sunken cheeks, darkened eyes, and bald head to see I was light years away from OK. My mom knew something was amiss, but the truth was so terrible that no normal human being could even begin to imagine what I was going through. What father would do such abominable things to their own child? What mother could guess at the atrocity?

And anyway, I'd had my chance to escape. On August 30, 1990, nearly ten months after the wall fell, I'd visited home.

It was a fast trip. My father had altered my tickets last minute, reducing the visit to just one week. School started the following week, and because of my fierce commitment to my education, he knew I wouldn't extend the trip and miss class. With the twenty-four hours of travel one way and jet lag, it felt like I arrived and was saying goodbye moments later.

Seeing my family felt like ripping open the wounds I'd tried hard to keep stitched and bandaged all these years. The infection oozing out of the lesions of trauma; me trying desperately to clean up the mess so they wouldn't see just how damaged I was. I made small talk and smiled brightly when they asked about America, but I could see my mom studying me in her quiet way, taking in all the words I wasn't saying. I felt the gaze of my aunt, uncle, and cousin, the accepting eyes of my grandfather, the sad, distant look of my grandmother. Were they buying my act? I couldn't tell. But I knew I needed them to. If I was going to return to America and make right the lie I'd been living for so long, make the pain count, make my dream happen . . . well, they had to believe everything was fine.

Still, I wanted nothing more than for my mom to see past the façade and say, "Luissa, something is not right back in America. I don't know what it is, but you may not go back. You must stay here."

But of course, mothers can't read minds. She didn't know. How could she when I did everything I could to protect her from my secret?

During that visit to my family home, when everyone was occupied elsewhere, I kneeled in the dark of my grandfather's bedroom, my elbows on his bed and head resting on my clasped hands, and cried with my whole body, like I was burying someone very loved, someone near and dear to me. I cried for the family I loved and the life I'd left. For the life I suffered with my father. The dreams I'd had before I left for America; the dreams I still held even within the hell I was living. I cried for my grandmother, my grandfather, my mother. My aunt, my uncle, my cousin. My best friend, Bîzu. Even Paul, whom I'd lost contact with years earlier, who to me represented hope and innocence.

I cried for myself, for the version of Luissa who had died all those years back on my nineteenth birthday and continued to die small deaths every day with my father. When I finally stood many minutes later, my tears had made a Rorschach design on my grandfather's handmade quilt, seeping and spreading across the burgundy cotton. My pain growing. My heart shattering.

I had made the mistake of my life going to America—staying in America—and I couldn't tell anyone. I couldn't stay home in Romania. I had to go back.

I felt, in that moment, and during those first years in America, like I was in no man's land. The constant, endless turmoil pulsed in my temple as tears dried on my cheeks. Everything was so messy, so degraded, so shattered. It was like a once beautifully crafted piece of art was mishandled and broke into pieces. I was trying to mend the art back together, but one could see the fine cracks, proof of its unfortunate journey. Nothing felt real anymore. I wanted to pick up the pieces of myself and finish mending the brokenness so I could become a doctor, make my family proud, and push this painful present into the past.

All I wanted was for everything to be normal again. But nothing was normal. I felt completely spent.

I stood from my grandfather's bed and wiped my face with my shirt collar. Looking around my grandfather's bedroom, I thought of his great hopes for me. He was the only one of my family members who supported me being in America because he wanted me to have a better life. He saw the United States as a land of hope and possibility. God, if he knew. He already wanted to kill my father for ruining my mother's life. If he only knew what he was doing to me . . .

I shook my head quickly and took a deep breath. No, he must never know. No one will ever know.

I would keep pushing the reality down, bottling it in, and keep going. I'd go through the motions of the hell I was in because I had to. The one thing that gave me hope was that someday I would be able to put this all behind me and be normal again: have a family of my own, a profession. Pick up the shatters and tatters of my life and mend myself, one piece at a time. I told myself that if I kept going, maybe this messy life would fade away.

A week after I arrived in Romania, I left again. Back to America. Back to hell.

—

Just as my father had promised, I had enrolled in school that fall of my first year in America with him, taking a full load of five classes—the most courses I was ever allowed to take at once. Now five years in, every single class was a fight. Almost nightly, my father would attack my dream: Why do you want to go to school? We don't have the money. Why not just work in the business?

But I was firm: I'm going to school. My father had stripped away nearly everything I had, but he couldn't take that. I was taking only one class per semester, working, taking care of all the household duties, and clawing at my dream as it was floating away from me moment by moment. Allowing me to enroll in school, even with the fighting, was enough to keep me believing that he was telling the truth about his intentions to help me become a doctor.

I held tight to the belief that, of all of this mess, at least one thing was true. In spite of the lies and abuse, he was still my father, after all. Doesn't every father want his daughter to be happy and successful?

This was one of the many lies I told myself to survive. I needed the lifeline, or I'd drown.

All day, every day, I kept moving. Work at one or more of my jobs. Grocery shopping, cooking, baking, cleaning, ironing. Class or studying at night. An inexpensive servant with a multitude of benefits for the master.

Working in my father's real estate business furthered my isolation. As soon as I got my green card and began learning written English, I started studying for my real estate license. I passed the salesperson exam in New Hampshire and then got my brokerage license one year later. I went further and passed the Maine and Massachusetts ones as well. I wanted his business to succeed so I could have money for college tuition. But the nature of working from a home office meant I was with my father for hours every day.

I had a desk in my bedroom where I would study, and a makeshift desk in the living area where I'd make the business phone calls and keep the books. When not at work in the grocery store, I spent most of my time at those desks or doing chores around the apartment, especially cooking.

While I did my best to keep the apartment bright and clean, I still wanted nothing more than to escape its walls. One walked into the kitchen straight from the front door of the apartment. The kitchen bordered the living room, with a two-person table and two chairs dividing the two rooms. It held a stove along one wall and a counter with the dishwasher under it and cabinets above, followed by a kitchen sink, a cabinet under it for storage and plumbing, and then the refrigerator. We never used the dishwasher because water and electricity cost money, so I washed all the dishes by hand.

The living room had a tiny closet on the left wall. Next to it was a trifold, double cot of beige-and-brown woven cloth that, during the day, would be stacked into a sitting couch, using the wall as a backrest. At night, it would be covered by sheets and a traditional handwoven Romanian blanket—that is where my father slept. The rectangular coffee table in the middle of the room was pushed to the side every night when the cot was made into a bed. On the opposite wall, there was a small television on a stand and a table that held an always-open Merriam-Webster dictionary and a typewriter. Next to the windows of the living area, at the opposite end of the apartment entrance, were a large wooden table (his desk), a potted hibiscus plant, and a small desk, which was my "office" desk.

Past the living room was a small bathroom containing a toilet and a bathtub with shower; Suzette's food and water bowls were set between the toilet and the cat litter box, which was under the bathroom sink. Next to the bathroom was a small closet, followed by the door to my bedroom.

My bedroom had one full-size bed with broken springs that poked me at night despite the blankets I put under the sheet. I slept covered with a traditional Romanian quilt given to my father from someone in his village, which I later replaced with one sent by my mom—a beautiful handmade satin goose-down comforter in white and violet. The bedroom had a small closet, one credenza, and a wall mirror. Next to the mirror was a copy machine for the real estate business, a student desk with a chair by the window, and potted hibiscus trees next to it.

This was the one-bedroom apartment I lived in for years. My prison.

I was only allowed to leave the apartment for work at the supermarket, with my father for real estate showings, to run errands, to attend school, to go running, or to take walks with Suzette. I had no friends. My coworkers and I moved past each other like ghosts, never interacting except for the essential communication our jobs required. A few coworkers had made an effort to be friends outside of work, but I had told them I was too busy to go out. At school, I distanced myself from my classmates, listening intently to lectures and then leaving immediately because I knew I'd be in trouble if I didn't arrive home when expected. In six years with my father, I'd never gone out with anyone other than him, except for the one time his younger brother visited us for a couple of days.

There was little rest. When I wasn't working, at school, or doing homework, I had endless domestic duties around the apartment. I baked, pickled, and cooked. I mended clothes, cleaned, did the laundry, and ironed my father's button-up dress shirts because he never wore T-shirts. I hated ironing his shirts. To this day, I hate ironing.

In Romania, I had been the princess of the house, hardly lifting a finger unless I wanted to please my family, especially my mom or grandmother. I'd been allowed to have a childhood, given the freedom to study, read, play, and rest.

But that life was long lost.

Sometimes, when washing the dishes or ironing a shirt or mopping the floor, the memories of home would overtake me, as if I were carried to another place and time, drifting across land and ocean to return to Romania.

I would remember walking the promenade with my mom or watching my grandfather spread salt across his massive cutting board. I'd think of my grandmother's gallbladder surgery, and how I had gotten up every day to make her breakfast. How I'd boil an egg or make fresh cheese from the unpasteurized milk we bought at the market. I'd remember the little details too: how I'd put the milk into a jar ahead of time so it became yogurt, then cook it slightly on the stove so it was hot but not boiling. How the cheese would float to the top and I'd pour the liquid over a strainer to collect it for breakfast, much like queso fresco. How my grandmother and I would sit together and enjoy the special breakfast I'd made.

I'd recall how I would make her bed while she was away at church or tidy the apartment just to see her face light up in gratitude. I'd think of how, before the hard times, I would surprise my mom with gifts from my own pocket money. I saved up cash from my grandfather on my birthday, from my neighbors while Christmas caroling with my cousin at their apartments, and from my grandfather on January 1, when we celebrated his given name, Saint Basil. Or I'd bring her a flower from the forbidden bushes, tucking a rose under my jacket while watching to make sure no one saw. Each time, each surprise, my mother would give me that smile she reserved just for me. Her Luissa. Her princess.

I had the luxury of these daydreams when I was alone. But of course, I wasn't often alone.

During these years with my father, I felt like I was living two selves. Two separate halves of a severed whole. There was the broken me who was desperately trying to survive my father. And then there was the Luissa I had been in Romania, the girl I took out of the box every Sunday to talk with my mom. These calls were the only time I felt safe and comfortable. Human. Like I could let my guard down as the Old Luissa.

There were very few things I refused to give up during those years with my father. Talking with my mom on Sundays was one of them, but like anything that gave me joy or meaning, I had to fight to keep it. He was against it—"such nonsense," he would bark at me. I started having panic attacks when I woke up on Sunday mornings. I would lie in bed, motionless, thinking about calling her. My heart would start racing and I would begin to sweat and feel out of breath. To calm myself down, I would tune my thoughts to the importance of hearing my mom's voice and how that would make me feel.

My father blamed fights about the calls on money, but in reality he felt threatened by my connection to my old life. So to keep my lifeline—my connection to my mom—I figured out that I could speak with her for fifty-nine seconds, hang up, and call back, continuing this for the duration of our calls. When the phone statement came, I would call the company and point out the duplicate charges for one minute, saying I'd been disconnected, blaming it on the quality of the international connections, and the company would then waive the fees. By doing so, I was able to talk with my mom without costing my father money.

I had to hear her voice to survive. It was a lifeline. I was drowning, grabbing on to anything that linked to my first life, to the people I loved, to the normalcy I longed for and could not have. I lived for these weekly Sunday phone calls and waited eagerly to receive my mom's letters, which she would write and send daily, even though only some of them would make it to me because of the combination of a poor mail system and the censorship in Romania. She would send small packages with clothes my grandmother knitted and crocheted for me just like when I was at home. When I talked with her each Sunday, I'd ask her advice. How do I make my favorite Christmas cake, *cozonac*? Can you send me the recipe for your *supă de găină* (chicken soup)? My mom would then mail me handwritten recipes. When they arrived, I'd take in her neat handwriting and wish I could wrap myself in her Os and Ds.

These calls and mail from my mom were my fortress walls that kept me from either becoming hopeless, going mad, being self-destructive, or worse.

And Suzette—Suzie—my furry friend, the only living creature allowed around me that loved me in her own way, helped keep Old Luissa from dying completely. I loved her with all my being.

Over time, I pieced together how to do each of the duties required of me in my new life. I learned how to make stuffed cabbage, stuffed grape leaves, chicken, and meatball soup. Pickled vegetables of all sorts. Pastries, Easter eggs, and *cozonac*. Cured pastrami, sausages, and cheese. My father taught me how to bake bread from scratch because he refused to buy bread. "It's laden with chemicals," he would say, just the same as with vending machines and restaurants. I would have appreciated the liberty to experiment and make my own decisions.

I learned how to fix the car, too, because my father wouldn't take the car into the shop because of money. I changed the oil, filters, spark plugs, and coolant, and replaced the brakes. Changed the bulbs. Fixed flats.

On top of these duties at home and in the business, I continued keeping the finances for the household, paying bills, and balancing the checkbook. Since he reviewed the bank statements to ensure I wasn't taking money, it never crossed my mind to forge a check to myself and cash it, or keep any of the money that came in.

Other than a few cooking tasks, my father did not contribute to the household except to tell me what needed doing or to be done better. I was not thanked. I was not recognized for my hard work or organization. There was never acknowledgment of the load I carried—financially, domestically, personally. Never.

And why would there be? My father didn't care for me. I was there to serve him.

This became especially clear when my father called my half-sister to talk to her. He would call her frequently—I considered anything "frequent" when compared with the once-a-year calls I would get from him when I was back in Romania. He would tell her repeatedly during each call how much he loved and missed her. He even carried her four-by-six-inch picture in his briefcase so everyone could see his daughter, my sister, when he opened the case.

One day, I listened to him talking with her, asking about what to get for her birthday, which was coming up. "Anything you want," he said. He sounded so sweet, so sincere, so fatherly toward her.

I waited until he hung up then asked him, "Why do you treat her like a true daughter? Why don't you treat me the same way? Why, father?"

"She is my daughter," he replied. "I raised her."

His words struck me like a slap. "What about me? Who am I to you then?

Am I not your daughter too?" I turned away from him, left the apartment, and fled to the cemetery, where I cried alone for a long time.

I was like a slave: isolated, totally financially dependent, and therefore at his will. I applied to get a credit card a couple of times, but I was declined because I had no credit. He made sure to remind me of these difficulties—that without him I was a nobody.

To the outside world, my father presented himself as a shining light of brilliance and family values. He referred to himself as Dr. Livius Fişteag—after Titus Livius, the famous Roman historian—even though I'd learn years later that he didn't finish his dissertation and was never awarded a doctorate. To present himself as a family man, he included pictures of the two of us in marketing collateral for the business. He offered classes through the Fişteag Institute, which no one ever signed up for. When we went to church, he presented himself as a caring father who was trying to make the world a better place for his daughter. Sometimes he would even take me to have a picnic at Bear Brook State Park or ski at Crotched Mountain in New Hampshire.

These father-like professions and efforts were confusing as I navigated the hell at home, where he was paranoid and jealous. Anything that took me outside the house, any connection I had, was a threat. Even with the abuse, I still couldn't understand why he wouldn't be supportive of my dream. I'd tell him: Parents would pay gold for their children to want so badly to go to school to better themselves. He always brought his objections back to money. But money was never the reason. He wanted to control me. I was his to use and abuse.

Sometimes I wonder if my father believed his own lies. Maybe he had to split himself in two just like I did, only while I did it to survive, he did it to live with himself.

Maybe he also lived with himself by allowing me the few joys in my life: school, phone calls with my mom, Suzie. Those phone calls and moments with Suzette allowed me to temporarily shed the skin of my abuse. But nearly every other hour of every day, I put Old Luissa back in her box in favor of New Luissa. Floating through my days, holding tight to Sunday calls with Mom and my dream to one day heal others as a doctor. Sometimes I felt like

I was full of helium, holding on to this earth by my index finger, grasping a tree branch, trying desperately not to float away.

Nothing was clear. Everything was muddy and messy. He deconstructed every single part of my life. Nothing was sacred. Nothing was secret. Nothing was mine.

Looking back on those years, I recognize now that I could have gone crazy. I could have killed myself or gone down a road of drugs or other ways of coping. So many horrible things could have happened. But instead, I separated myself in two, keeping the old me in a metaphorical safe, preserving the self I'd brought to America, distancing from the self who had to survive the abuse of my father. Somewhere deep inside, I must have known I would someday reunite the parts of myself to become whole.

8

$1,000 FOR FREEDOM

I lay in bed on the fifth floor of Massachusetts General Hospital, moving my fingers gently on the mass in my abdomen. The hospital hummed just outside my door: beds being wheeled past my room; the drifting sound of a phone ringing and a voice talking into the receiver; elevator doors dinging over and over, bringing patients, visitors, and staff here and there.

I was scheduled for surgery that day. Looking around the two-person room I had to myself, my gaze rested on the view outside the window next to my bed, taking in the spring green color of the trees in the distance. I felt the deep ache of loneliness. No one was there; no one would be there. My father had dropped me off the day before, rushing back to the apartment and far away from the hospital as soon as he could. My family was a world away, dealing with their own ache: the loss of my grandfather.

When I thought of my sweet grandfather, my gut felt hollow, like someone had scooped out my insides and I now held cavernous guilt within me. My mom had called two weeks earlier to tell me of his passing. He had been ill with pancreatic cancer, and while he had been dying for some time, the loss didn't hurt any less.

With just three days to the burial, I told my mom I couldn't afford the travel. Instead, I would grieve him here in America, my strong Bunicu, who had become a changed man so suddenly and irreversibly for me. It distressed me to be away from my family during such a difficult time, when we needed to be together and celebrate the life of the man who had been the rock and compass of our family. The man who loved us each unconditionally, who wanted nothing more than for his dear Luissa to thrive in America as a doctor.

What I didn't tell my mom was that it wasn't just the money that kept me away. I was too sick to travel.

A couple months prior, in early spring 1992, I was studying to take the Medical College Admission Test, the all-important MCAT I needed to take to apply to medical school. While I hadn't yet fulfilled the bachelor's degree requirement, I had completed all the required pre-med classes. Combined with a near-perfect test score, my father said—and I confirmed by reading the paperwork myself—I would meet the minimum requirement to be admitted to medical school. My English was getting better, and I had passed the test required for nonnative English speakers with flying colors. I was grasping all the scientific and mathematical knowledge in English and felt confident I would do well on the MCAT. After all, American tests were so easy compared to Romanian tests.

Even with a high test score, however, no medical school would have admitted me. There is a highly competitive pool of applicants every year, typically all of whom have bachelor's degrees, some of whom even have dual degrees and master's degrees. Just because it was remotely possible on paper that I could be admitted didn't mean it was possible in real life. This false hope was another of my father's strategic moves to keep me placated. But at the time, the knowledge that I could take the test and apply to medical school kept me above water.

Around this time, I started noticing a lump in my abdomen disrupting the contour of my belly. I felt the mass only when I was lying down, and I blamed it on the coffee, stress, and constipation I'd been experiencing. I began checking it nightly, pushing the mass around; if I pressed it downwards, it would pop back up again, always coursing the same, from the lower left to upper right of my abdomen. It was painless, mobile, and growing—in fact, it felt rather large, like I had a baseball in my gut. As it grew, I grew more worried.

Weeks passed. One night, I got up to go to the bathroom and couldn't empty my bladder. After several minutes of straining, to no avail, I realized the mass must be pressing on my bladder and preventing me from emptying it. Desperate, I lay on the ground and did leg raises, thinking that whatever was pressing my insides would move around and off my bladder—and I was eventually able to use the bathroom.

I knew something was very wrong. This couldn't be normal.

The next day, I told my father I needed to go to the doctor. Instead, he took me to the pharmacy and homeopathic store, where he bought herbs and senna seeds. After taking in liters of herbal tea for a few days and gulping down the soaked gooey senna concoctions, my symptoms continued to worsen. I could hardly eat because of intense nausea and had to continue my leg lifts nightly to be able to use the bathroom. When I insisted again that I needed to be checked by a real doctor, my father brushed me off.

"We don't have insurance. And I don't have the money to take you to see doctors, get tests, or have procedures," he said. "Besides, these doctors are all hacks. The more they do to you, the more they make." He then proceeded to tell me about the time when he lost his voice because of a parakeet allergy and was told he may have throat cancer, another time he was told he might have stomach cancer when it was actually an ulcer, and yet another time when a doctor said he may have to lose a kidney when he just had kidney stones.

"Keep taking the herbs," he said. "You'll be fine."

But I knew I wasn't going to be fine. The mass was growing and so was the intense nausea and constipation. I started researching, attempting to shed light on this mystery mass and the possible diagnosis. I began to panic, my reasoning homing in on the word "cancer."

Desperate, I looked into buying tickets to Romania, where I could get free medical care. But last-minute tickets were too expensive, and I had no way to get international travel papers on such a tight timeline, so I knew I needed to push my father to take me in. Once again, I was stuck. Powerless.

As the nausea grew worse, I took a pregnancy test even though I'd already had my period.

Finally, I became so nauseated I couldn't eat at all except for broth and water-rich fruits. The only time I didn't feel sick was while running. So even though I was fatigued, I ran twice per day, sighing in relief as the pressure in my abdomen released and dreading when I would have to stop my run and the intense discomfort would return. I lost about 20 pounds—which was a lot considering I only weighed 115 pounds to begin with—my cheeks sinking further into my face, my skin pale. After weeks of my suffering, my father finally took me to a doctor. I was to miss the MCAT I'd studied so hard to take.

It only took the doctor one look to see I was unwell and in distress, bordering on cachexia—weakness and wasting of the body due to severe chronic illness. After listing my symptoms, he sent me back to have an X-ray; later, he led me into a quiet exam room to discuss the results.

"You have a dermoid cyst," he told me.

"A what?"

"A dermoid cyst," he repeated. "It's a mass in your belly."

"Dermoid cyst," I echoed. My relief at having a diagnosis was instantly replaced with fear of the outcome. "I've never had this before . . . why . . . when . . .?"

"It's in your left ovary. It has been growing for a while. Probably years."

Years.

The years I'd been with my father.

"You need to go to the hospital," he said. His voice softened as he added, "You'll need it surgically removed. I'll give you a referral."

As he wrote the prescription, he explained what was growing inside me. When humans are formed as embryos, there are three layers: ectoderm, endoderm, and mesoderm. Ecto means outside, endo means inside, and meso means middle. Dermoid cysts contain all three layers, are mostly benign in origin, and contain within them teeth, hair, skin, cartilage, and sebaceous, or wax-secreting, glands. A cyst of this size can twist and cause the adjacent ovary to die and rupture, causing contents to leak into the abdomen, leading to infection, bleeding, shock, and death. I had, in essence, a noncancerous, nonliving creature within me.

As my father drove me from Manchester to Massachusetts General Hospital that day, I sat silently in the car next to him, thinking over the past years. I had started losing my hair a few years earlier—was that connected to my cyst? When I'd had the abortions—was the cyst growing? It was like I had a body invader that grew with my isolation and pain, a not-child of the trauma I was experiencing every day with my father.

We arrived at Massachusetts General and my doctor, Dr. May, a small-framed, confident OB-GYN, did an abdominal ultrasound and attempted a pelvic exam. But she couldn't even get the speculum in because the mass was pushing against so much of my organs and the lower pelvis. After examining me and seeing how sick I was, she decided I needed surgery right away. Prior to surgery, she ordered several blood tests to rule out possible types of ovarian cancers. She would take a biopsy of the mass during surgery to check for cancer.

My father continued to push against me having the surgery until the very last moment, calling the whole thing a scam and the doctors money-hungry crooks. He instead wanted me to give the herbs time to work some miracle.

On April 21, 1992, I woke up from surgery alone. I hadn't told anyone about the procedure. Only my father knew, and he had already left the hospital, heading back to his apartment and far away from my suffering. I had no family nearby and no friends. I was utterly alone, with a midline incision from my sternum to my symphysis pubis, an IV in my arm, and deep sadness aching within me. I wanted nothing more in that moment than for my mom to hold my hand, rub my cheek, and tell me everything would be OK. I wanted to be with my family, to mourn my grandfather, to feel wrapped in love like I'd been in Romania. Instead, I blinked my eyes in the too-bright hospital room and moaned from the pain, hoping that the thing that had caused me so much discomfort was forever gone and I would be OK.

When my miracle woman—my doctor—came in to see me later that day, she brought good news. It was not cancer. It was a benign cyst weighing 2.2 pounds. They had removed it and placed it into a jar, whole. I asked the doctor if I could keep it. She said she didn't know why not.

Then, she shared the bad news. I had lost one ovary because my fallopian tube had been so engulfed in the mass and it strangulated the ovary in the process, cutting its blood supply. But my other ovary was functioning fine and I would be able to get pregnant someday if I wanted to. Unfortunately, she added, there was a 5 percent chance of recurrence on the remaining ovary.

Over the next days, I began to feel exponentially better. When my doctor stopped in to check on me, she'd ask how I was doing. My answer, seemingly on a loop: "I'm hungry."

Her ongoing question: "Is your gut making noises?"

"No, not yet."

"Well, we must wait. Your gut is still asleep."

After two days, a shy but definite noisy action in my tummy interrupted the silence of my hospital room. I called in the nurse and cried, "My belly is awake!"

I was finally allowed to eat. Chicken broth and apple sauce for lunch, chicken soup with rice and chocolate ice cream for dinner. Who says hospital food is not the best? Food never tasted so good in my entire life.

Now several days post-operation, I was going to be released later that day. I would go back to my life with my father. But at least I would be well—not so helpless anymore, not so defenseless. I ached not just from the surgery but from going through it alone, without even one person by my side or one person calling to check on me. The sorrow was amplified by the loss of my grandfather, who I never really got a chance to mourn. Who, as I lay on the floor of my father's apartment in agony, had died. Who had left this earth believing that his Luissa was safe and happy. That she was living a dream life in America and making our family proud.

If he knew.

If he only knew.

Two weeks later, once I was certain I was going to be OK, I called my mom to tell her about the surgery. In her stunned silence on the other end of the line, I could hear her shock at my secrecy. She questioned me over and over: "Why? Why didn't you call? Why didn't you tell me?"

I told her it was because of Grandpa, and in part, it was. I didn't want to burden her. I didn't want my pain to become hers, or for my family to carry more than they could bear during a time of loss and mourning. As true as that was, I also worried that, in my vulnerability, I would reveal more of my life in America. I couldn't let that happen. My family must never know. Just like I suffered alone with my cyst, I would suffer alone through this trial of my soul. And only when I had survived, when I came through to the other side, would I let my family know a fraction of the hardship I endured.

I promised my mom I would write her a detailed letter of my health saga, and I sure did. But of course, I focused the retelling on the medical situation, not the life with my father that led me to that hospital room.

I could never share the full story.

Never.

With distance, with the wisdom of today, with the perspective of a healed woman looking in on her twenty-something self in that room, alone, I see so much that I did not see back then. The cyst, a metaphor for the trauma growing within me. The empty room, my cavernous soul. The loss of my grandfather, a shattered dream of reuniting with my Romanian roots. Of being normal again. Of not being broken but instead being whole and complete, like I was before.

—

It wasn't until more than a year later, in November 1993, that I would see my mom for the second time in the seven years I lived with my father. And during that two-week trip to Romania, something began to shift inside me. I visited friends, strolled along the Danube River esplanade, and even ventured into Constanța to visit Padre at his new parish. I admired the parade of roses on Karl-Marx Boulevard and breathed in memories of my childhood. But most of all, I felt the cocoon of my family deeply, the safety of their presence, the ability to fall asleep at night filled with peace and safety.

And yet I still carried the burden of my true life with my father. Shame sat on my shoulder in every conversation, every hug. It whispered in my ear, "You have to make this right." In my skewed thinking, I believed it was my mistake coming to America, staying in America. Even though I was barely an adult when I arrived in the United States, I blamed myself for believing my father, for giving up my country and my mom, all for my dream of becoming a doctor. I had to fix the mess that was my life. Nobody else.

And I believed that maybe I still could. Two things would shift everything: receiving my American citizenship and attending medical school. These goals were close, just beyond the reach of my outstretched palm, almost near enough to grasp tightly and never let go. While medical school was further away, I knew I was tenacious enough to become the doctor I'd dreamed of since fifth grade.

It was like I was running a marathon and, while I'd hit roadblock after roadblock, I knew I was destined to reach the finish line. A marathon, like any endurance sport, is a mind game. You can train to reach your peak performance as a runner. But you can't finish a race solely based on your trained body; it's only through the power of your mind that you can complete all 26.2 miles. You must train your mind to accept, embrace, and endure this arduous effort to reap the reward of crossing the finish line. You bow your head, your sweat drips, your muscles ache, and a voice in your mind whispers, "You can do this!" You remain in control of only what you can control, adapt to the situation at present, and keep your eyes on the prize. The pain fades to the background as you focus only on the goal ahead.

In my case, my father took almost everything away from me. But the walls I had raised within my soul were built out of something stronger than brick and mortar and meant to protect the single most beautiful seedling left: hope. A belief that one day I could achieve the only dream left unbroken, unspoiled, unhurt. These walls were built out of my beautiful childhood and adolescence in Romania, the daily normalcy, the simple truths, the sun's bright light, the wishes made with every New Moon—*Craiul Nou*. The multicolored, fragrant roses I strolled by, the green of the trees I rested under, the dewy grass I walked on barefoot by the riverbanks of the Danube, the church mass songs I prayed, the "Habanera" aria I hummed, the carefree laughs, and the peaceful dreamy nights. All these experiences intertwined with the love poured over me for the first eighteen years and eleven months of my life in Romania to keep me from crumbling. And once everything seemed lost, I created anchors in my new life: the fifty-nine-second lifelines with Mom, the letters, the recipes, the college classes, my little Suzette, the two brief trips home. These experiences continued to feed my living walls to keep me sane, focused, and hopeful. This was meant to be my walk through the valley of the shadows, and I would make it to the other side.

While citizenship and medical school wouldn't wash me clean, perhaps I could at least free myself from the torment of the past seven years. Free myself from my father.

One day, toward the end of my trip, my mom called me into the bedroom I'd shared with her and my grandma as a child. I entered the room with a smile, taking in her short, slender frame and narrow face with wrinkles around her eyes that had deepened during my time away, adorned by blond, curly hair with streaks of gray. I held childhood memories of my time in this room tenderly: my mom brushing my curls back and kissing my forehead before bed; my grandma bringing me a glass of water before bed; my grandpa tucking me in, pushing the covers tight around me and gingerly pinching my neck, calling me his little obléț.

My mom was sitting on the bed, clutching an envelope to her torso with both hands.

"Sit down," she said in Romanian, patting the spot next to her.

As soon as I sat down, she held the envelope toward me. Even though she wore a smile, her sky-blue eyes weren't smiling. She seemed tense. Worried.

"*Ce este asta?*" What's this? I asked, cautiously taking the thick envelope.

"*Sînt bani, dolari.*" It's money, dollars.

"*Bani?*"

"$1,000."

I handed the envelope back to her. "*Mami nu pot lua de la tine—*" Mom, I can't take this from you—

She pushed it away gently. "*Tu trebuie.*" You must.

Warmth rose from my stomach to my chest. I couldn't accept this money from my mom. After all, I was the one who was supposed to be supporting *her*, not the other way around. I lived in America! The most prosperous country in the world! The land of opportunity!

I felt the hotness of tears forming in my eyes as I met my mom's gaze. "Why?" I asked in Romanian.

"Because you might need it, Luissa," she replied. "I want you to take this money and put it somewhere safe." Her instructions were implied: Hide it from your father.

"But Mom—"

"Luissa. Listen to me. I spoke with your father before you came."

I breathed in sharply as she went on.

"I asked why he'd allowed you to get so sick and why it was taking so long for you to go to medical school." She paused and turned her entire body toward me, her left knee leaning on the bed so she could place her hands on my knees. "He said to me, 'Luissa will never become a doctor. She is here to take care of me. She will, however, make a very good secretary for our business.'"

My breath escaped quickly, like someone had punched me in the gut, hard. All this time, my father had no intention of me achieving my goal. How could I be so naïve? Of all his lies, all his betrayal, all his abuse, how could I have expected that this one thing would be true?

My dream. The only thing that had kept me going all these years . . . it was a lie? I suddenly felt like I was going to be sick or black out. My ears rang as though I'd been thrown underwater. Sweat began to bead on my arms and face. I closed my eyes and took a deep breath.

Steady, I told myself. Steady. Mom must never know.

When I opened them a few seconds later, my mom was watching me, her eyebrows drawn tight and her eyes shining with the threat of shared tears.

My mom took my hands in hers. "Please. Please take it. Just take it and keep it, just in case something comes up that you need it for."

I stared at the envelope now sitting in my lap. My mom's handwriting on the front: Luissa. The carefully sealed flap. My mom's love tucked inside in the form of $1,000 in American bills.

As I accepted my mom's gift, the tears I'd held back for so many years released. I wept, not just for the pain I suffered back home but also for my mother, who was unaware of my suffering and of the true value of the gift she had just given me. And I cried from shame, because I felt my mom never should have had to make such a great sacrifice for me. In 1993, that $1,000 was a fortune to her, especially in the struggling Romanian economy.

How did she know? She couldn't have any idea of my father's abuse, but how had she seen that I needed a lifeline?

While I thought I had hidden my distress from my family, a mother always knows. She saw her daughter's bald head and dark eyes. She knew I'd gotten so ill that I had barely eaten for three weeks and had been hospitalized. She knew I wasn't the same Luissa, that the brightness within me had dimmed so much it was nearly out, that the curly-haired belle of the ball had transformed into a skinnier, quieter version of her daughter.

"I'm supposed to help you," I whispered. "You're not supposed to be the one helping me."

"You are my daughter," she said. "I will always help you." She leaned over to wrap me in her strong arms, as I heaved and shuddered my last tears.

"*Mami, sărut mîna,*" I finally said. "*Sărut mîna.*" Mom, thank you. Thank you.

I held her then, grasping her small frame and wishing I never had to let go.

—

On the flight home from Romania, I checked the pocket of my jacket at least two dozen times, feeling the thick envelope safely tucked away, the wad of cash representing hope and safety. I didn't know when I'd use it, or how, but I knew it was a lifeline.

During the twenty-four hours of travel back to America, I couldn't help running through my life and decisions over the last six and half years. Why hadn't I left long before? Why hadn't I run at the first assault or the first broken promise—when my father refused to bring my mother to America so many years earlier?

Nothing was clear to me during those years, in the thick of the experience, in the alternate reality that is trauma, trying to just get by day by day, desperately maintaining the dying whisper of dignity and hope.

The truth is that I had retreated into myself to protect against the reality I was confronting. Rather than fight or flight, I froze. On my nineteenth birthday, my logical brain went at least partially offline and my emotional brain took over, triggering a fear response that kept me in a cycle of abuse for all those years. Alone on an island with my enemy and a cat as my only friend.

But something about the money my mom gave me woke me from the stupor of trauma. It was like I suddenly had fuel for flight, like I'd been given a gift that made leaving possible. With my American citizenship on the horizon, this money provided the practical tool I needed to be able to make it on my own in America.

As my plane landed in Boston, I thought of the first day I'd arrived on American soil, with my red windbreaker and white shoes, and a small suitcase containing what I needed for a short stay in America. I had carried hope—to know my father, to discover more about myself. I had everything then: a family, friends, a network of influence, a bright future awaiting me.

But within weeks, I had nothing. After filing for political asylum, I was without a country. I didn't know a soul. I couldn't speak the language, which is one of the biggest barriers anyone can experience. By default, America was my only choice unless I fled to another country, alone. I had no money except the $1 a week allowance my father eventually gave me once I started bringing in money.

For years now, I had tried to get a credit card to give me some financial breathing space. Every time, I was turned away because I didn't have a credit score. And since everything was in my father's name, I also didn't have a bank account. I had started to lose hope that I would ever have enough money to leave my father.

Now, I would be an American citizen soon. Although it felt like a mirage at times, I was on my way to medical school. I had finally formed one solid friendship at Market Basket with a woman named Kim. I was fluent in English. And I had $1,000 to fund my escape.

The money my mom gave me was an impetus for freedom. It, along with hearing my father's intentions for my professional future, was my trigger to leave—a moment when the veil of my abuse was dropped, when I suddenly had agency.

My goal of graduating medical school was a lifeline that enabled me to survive each day with my father. I clung desperately to my dream—it held a flicker of hope, the bright green seedling that remained undamaged in spite of the daily torment I experienced. I saw donning a white coat as my ticket to normal, an achievement that would allow me to put this hell behind me and eventually have a respectable life as a physician, reunite with Mom here in America, and have a husband, children, and a home of our own. When I became a doctor, I reasoned, I would finally be able to free myself.

My mother's generosity stirred something within me that enabled me to envision a sooner escape. Maybe I didn't need to become a doctor before I could leave. Maybe I could do it sooner, on my own.

Maybe I could make a choice to not suffer any longer. To take action. Maybe I could rise up . . . and finally open wide my sprouting, bright wings and fly. Free.

9

FREEZE, THEN FLIGHT

My life began again when I received my American citizenship on December 3, 1993. For the first time in my life, I felt I had accomplished something in the United States, in my new country.

The night before, I kept waking up, eyeing the alarm clock next to my bed. At about six in the morning, I finally gave up. I got out of bed, dressed, and went for my usual three-mile run along the railway tracks and through the cemetery—my daily reflection time through the places that kept me company. When I returned, I greeted Suzette, who was waiting at the door for me as part of our daily ritual, and played an abridged version of hand-cat roughhousing. Then I quickly showered and dressed, and out the door I went.

I had watched the weather channel the night before: no snow or sleet in the forecast. A sunny, cold winter day. Fine with me. With about a forty-five-minute drive ahead of me, I left with plenty of time for traffic and got there fifteen minutes early for the ceremony set to start at nine o'clock that morning.

I was sworn in with a group of twenty-five other people at the State House in Concord, New Hampshire. I was there by myself. No friends, no family, no relatives. My father was not in attendance because he had chosen that week to travel to Romania for the second time since I'd arrived. His absence was a blessing. I did not want him there. His presence would have spoiled the sanctity of that experience, of all I had overcome to reach the moment when I, Luissa Daniela Vrâncuţa, became a citizen of the United States of America.

I wore my best outfit to the ceremony, a cream button-down blouse with crochet ruffles at the neck and sleeves, a fitted navy-blue skirt, and navy-blue high-heel shoes. As I raised my right hand to accept my new country of citizenship, I felt anew.

There were a lot of others like me there, from many countries, all coming together to claim our place as citizens of the United States of America. Along with the others, I recited the Oath of Allegiance, swearing to honor my new country, to uphold its laws and defend it when required. As I recited those words, I felt a sense of relief wash over me. I became an American citizen, and now, I was an entity. Before, I had nothing. I was stateless. Now, I belonged somewhere.

It's strange to reflect on this with distance. Here I was, living in America for almost seven years, and yet I barely knew anything about this vast country, its people, its systems, or its customs. My biggest barrier when I had moved there, language, wasn't a barrier anymore. When I started learning English those first months in America, I began to practice by replying to my father in English instead of Romanian, which frustrated him and caused him to complain about the American system, its people, and capitalism. I would reply, "You always complain about America. If you hate it that much, then you should go back to Romania."

Immersion in this new language quickly deepened as I started working outside the apartment at various grocery stores or while showing houses. Having a multilingual education from childhood—born into Romanian, French since second grade, German from fifth grade—my brain quickly started connecting the common words between these languages and understanding the gist of conversations by inference.

Before I moved to America, I was a dynamic, outspoken, witty, quicksilver young woman. The first few years in this new land, I became shy, quiet, self-conscious of my shortcoming—the new language barrier. But timidness wasn't me at the core. Now that I had language, I was starting to uncover the quicksilver within me.

While I had been readily absorbing the language, I'd never absorbed my father's distaste for the place and people. Even though my arrival there had brought with it immense pain, I felt no hate or bitterness toward this new country of mine. Why would I hate America? I hated my immature gullibility in believing in the stranger I called Father. I hated wasting almost seven years of my young life, with nothing to show for it, and missing out on so many things: opportunities, friendships, memories, life.

But to hate America? That was a firm no.

No longer was I a woman without a country. I had a country now. I had America.

—

As I promised loyalty to my country, the seed of resistance against my father, which had been planted during my last trip to Romania, grew. I'd felt for so many years like a bird with clipped wings who wanted desperately to fly. With American citizenship, my mom's generous financial gift, and the knowledge of my father's deceit and intentions, it was like my wings had been restored, the window open before me. No longer a dog locked in a cage but instead a bird ready to be free. And with my father out of the country, I knew it might be my only opportunity to escape the open cage to my future.

I had spent almost seven years frozen under his abuse. I was ready to fly.

But to survive on my own, I knew I needed three things: money to support myself, a place to live, and a car. My father only had a couple of weeks left of his trip, so I knew I needed to act quickly. Everything had to be ready before he arrived home. I had my paperwork for the US passport ready to go, so immediately after receiving my American citizenship, I headed to the post office and met with a clerk, who verified I had everything to process my passport.

The clerk eyed my brand-new naturalization certificate. "You're not wasting any time," she said, placing it carefully in the envelope with the application.

Panic rose within me. I didn't realize I had to send in my certificate. "Can you just use a copy instead?" I said.

"Nope," she said calmly. "It must be the original."

"But, I—I just got it. What if it gets lost?"

"Don't worry. It won't. Here, I'll make you a copy."

Moments later, she handed me an ugly, black-and-white version of my newly earned treasure. With a sigh, I thanked her and left, resigning myself to a poor replica of my citizenship. On the bright side, I thought, I had made the next huge step toward my freedom. Once I had my American passport, nothing would limit my ability to go home to my family.

Next, I readied myself to leave my father. I started by approaching the store manager at Market Basket, where I had started as a bagger and quickly advanced to cashier when my English improved. I had been there for years and was a loyal employee, but they hadn't given me full-time hours because it would require them to provide health insurance and other benefits. Plus, I had been working for my father's business and hadn't had the extra time to work more. At the end of a shift the day after I received my citizenship, I told my manager I needed to move out, and to do so, I'd need full-time hours. Could he do that for me? Could he provide enough hours that I would be able to support myself? He agreed and mentioned that the assistant front-end manager was leaving. If I was interested, the position—and the raise coming with it—was mine. With an enthusiastic "yes," I gave him a big hug and thanked him over and over. Being able to cover my own bills was another step toward independence.

I then set about the next item on my list: finding a car. My only friend, Kim, and I went to Nashua to go car shopping. Kim knew nothing of the true situation with my father, except that I wanted to move out and needed her help. We'd met at Market Basket and over the last months had slowly formed a friendship. While she didn't probe too much into my circumstances and had no idea of the extent of my misfortune, she'd gathered enough from our past conversations to know my life wasn't rosy. She knew I needed to move out and get my own space and was glad to help me. Getting a car, I knew, would be one of my greatest hurdles because I needed a loan. Throughout the many years I'd applied for credit cards and personal loans, I'd never been approved. Would the bank come back again saying I didn't have credit, so I couldn't get credit?

I knew my freedom hinged on having transportation. A few years after arriving in the country, I'd finally been allowed to get my driver's license when my father lost his because of lack of car insurance and he needed someone to drive him around. But to have my own car . . . well, that would feel like freedom. Plus, there was no way I could get to work and school in a timely manner taking public transportation—shifts and classes were often scheduled nearly back-to-back—and I also knew that owning a car would provide me with freedom and autonomy. After a full day of shopping, I fell in love with a red 1993 Oldsmobile Achieva. I put down a deposit of $100, applied for a loan of $11,500 at 7.9 percent interest through the dealership, and left, hoping I would get the car.

I worried all evening and into the next morning. What if I didn't get the loan? I had no one to vouch for me. No one to cosign. I was young, single, and with nobody to spot me. Would they overlook all those things to give me my freedom?

The next afternoon, the dealership called: My loan had been approved! Another domino had fallen in my favor, in what was beginning to feel like a cascade of good fortune that began with my mom's generosity. It was Friday and I would pick my car up the following Monday. Frantically, I started working to secure an insurance policy. And I did.

While I was getting my new life in order, I was also enjoying myself. With my father gone, I was able to stay out late with Kim, going to disco clubs and dancing until the early hours of the morning. I met a boy, Colt, whom I instantly liked. Kim and I went out nearly every night, and she arranged for us to meet up with Colt again, who asked for my number. We started talking on the phone and even met up after a work shift. I was falling for him.

These experiences of freedom let loose the dam within me, the pain that had kept me frozen flooding out of my body. I experienced normalcy for the first time in nearly seven years. What it was like to have friends, to dance, to like a boy. To go where I wanted, when I wanted. To own a car. To have money and control over my finances.

With my newly acquired transportation, I started looking for apartments in Nashua and found one in Boulder Park, a complex near the supermarket and the highway. The place had one bedroom, a living room, a kitchen, and one bathroom. The rent: $535 monthly, a small fortune to me but also a small price to pay for my freedom. It was clean, bright, and most importantly, it could be mine.

I needed to put down a $100 deposit and then come up with the first and last month's rent so I could move in less than a month later. Not wanting to lose my chance, I went ahead with the deposit knowing I had to come up with the remaining $1,070 quickly.

Wow! The sweet taste of being the master of my own actions, my life, my future—it was an amazing feeling. Words can't fully explain how I felt. Just like a beautiful sunrise photographed from atop a cliff, a photo won't fully capture the sunrise experienced in the moment: breathtaking, unique, never duplicated.

I was not healed, but I was free for those weeks without my father. And there was no way I was ever going back. I had left my cage and I would not return.

Finally, all I could do was wait. I had done everything I needed to do to ensure my freedom from my father. But I wasn't just going to flee in the night. I couldn't have closure if I didn't confront him.

My father would be home soon. I would pick him up from the airport. I would drive him back home, where I'd hand him the letter I'd written, telling him I was leaving. For all the confidence I'd found those past several days, the thought of seeing my father again made me physically nauseous. What would he do? Would he yell? Throw something? Play "nice father" to try to convince me to stay? I wasn't sure what his reaction would be, but the one thing I knew for sure: Nothing could make me stay. In my mind, I was already free.

A couple of days later, I picked my father up from the airport, driving his car because I didn't have the courage to drive my own, knowing he would have made a scene in the airport parking lot. His flight was delayed, and when he exited customs, I could see he was irate. Right away, he started yelling, telling me airport customs had taken the cured meats from his suitcase. I said nothing as he screamed and cursed the entire way to the car.

On the drive home, he noticed that something was off with me and asked what was wrong. I said I just didn't feel well, that I'd had a stomachache for about six days, and I didn't want to talk. As I drove distractedly, missing my exit once, my father complained about his family in Timișoara, saying everyone back home had given him a hard time and no one wanted to help him organize a political party. He continued to believe that communism wasn't entirely gone. His goal was to start his own grassroots political party and he needed his relatives' backing and especially their finances. I felt my stomach tighten as I grew more irritated by the minute, chiding myself for missing the exit and prolonging the drive.

Finally, he stopped talking and turned his body toward me.

"What is going on with you?" he said in Romanian.

I kept my eyes on the freeway. "I told you. I don't feel good."

"Something else is going on."

"No."

"What do you mean, 'no'?"

"I mean no, nothing is wrong."

The more aggravated he became that he couldn't make me talk, the more relaxed I became.

When we got home, I parked next to my car. As he retrieved his suitcase from the trunk and started to walk toward the stairs to his apartment, I stopped him and gestured toward my Oldsmobile.

"Father, what do you think of my new car?" I said. "I bought it while you were away."

He said nothing, turned back toward the building, and walked on.

Once we were in his apartment, I went to my bedroom and withdrew the letter from my desk. I held the folded sheets of paper in both hands, staring down at it for several seconds before lifting my chin and walking back into the living room, where my father was sitting in his recliner, wine on the side table next to him. I handed the letter out toward him.

"*Ce este asta?*" he said. What is this?

"*Te rog citește-o.*" I replied. Please read it.

He glowered at me but took the paper as instructed. After reading the first few lines, he threw it to the ground in disgust.

I stared at the pages scattered on the floor, stooping down to gather them, thinking of all I'd said in those pages—the conditions I was setting from here on out. That he was going to let me go to school full time, four to five courses per semester, so I could finish my bachelor's degree in two years. That he would let me have my own life and my own friends, with no questions and no conditions, because I was an adult and he couldn't rule me anymore. And finally, that except for $400 of rent that I would pay to live in his apartment until the end of the month, the rest of the money I earned would come directly to me.

And there was another condition if he wanted us to ever maintain some form of relationship as father and daughter: that I was no longer willing to accept his abuse. I gave him these conditions fully knowing he would never accept them.

I took a breath and stood, willing myself to look at him. Just then, the phone rang.

When I answered it, Colt was on the other line.

"Hi, Colt," I said.

My father looked aghast toward me. I excused myself and hung up.

"Who is Colt?" he demanded.

"He's my boyfriend."

Fury flashed across his face and he stood, his eyebrows wild and eyes wide.

"You sent me to Romania on purpose!" Spit flew from his mouth as he yelled. "You wanted to get rid of me! You wanted someone to kill me there!"

I willed myself to breathe evenly. "No, Father. I did not." I held the pages out to him again. "Just read the letter."

He snatched the letter from my hand and turned away from me, finally reading the words I'd written him in Romanian.

My dear father,

You may wonder why I wrote to you instead of talking to you. If I try to speak to you, there would be no use because we'd end up in a fight and I really do not want that. I want to explain to you some things and the decisions I had to make and what the alternatives are to them. There will be no feeling sorry, no tears. There will be only the truth and nothing but the truth.

You know that the lack of freedom, and everything you've done to me in the past six years and eight months, made me move further and further away from you. When I came here, I never loved you. I didn't even know you. You were a stranger to me, and then, I tried very, very hard to have patience. Two months ago, I realized that there is no interest on your part to let me finish my school; that it is taking an unreasonable amount of time, and then I started thinking of my alternatives.

I want you to understand that, in a way, I care about you because you are my biological parent, but nothing else and nothing more.

I went home and my mom had questions for me that I had to settle with her. She told me to have patience if I can and, if not, to do what I feel is best. Owning a car was imperative to me, and Mom, when she heard I had no money of my own, gave me $1,000. With that money, I bought, on December ninth, a car, an Oldsmobile, for an $11,500 loan. I want to assure you that nothing, no penny, of yours was used for this. What is more important, I have a car and you had never let me have one. So I did this on my own, with my own hands and my own mind.

Then I thought about finishing my school. But you'd never let me take a fair number of courses so I can finish school in a viable amount of time. Because you didn't even want me to finish anything, because you didn't want me to have a future, my own life, and to leave you behind.

So, I don't feel like I have to ask your permission to leave. One very important thing is that I have a friend. Yeah, a boy-friend. And believe you me, I am not going to pick between your fathership and his friendship.

He's twenty-six years old. His name is Colt. We like each other. We've been seeing each other for about two weeks, and it appears we are getting along fine.

This being said, these are the decisions that I came up with. If you want me to share the same roof with you until I get my own place, then all, and I say <u>ALL</u>, these conditions have to be accepted by you.

Starting January 1994, I will be taking at least four college courses per semester, enrolled as a full-time student in a major of my preference.

Next, I will be allowed to do anything that I desire with no interdictions of any kind in my life and in my freedom. I am young and no longer imprisoned. If I want to meet my friends or Colt anytime I want, anywhere, you cannot follow me nor will you restrict me. I will never sacrifice another day of my life for you, for your cause, for your business, anything. I am twenty-five years and seven months and I live my life without your help.

All the money that I am going to earn from working for you as a secretary or at Market Basket will be given to me as salary clearly established ahead of time.

As for alternatives, there are only two. All these decisions, all these demands must be accepted, respected, and signed by you, in writing. There is no negotiation or half acceptance involved. You accept everything or nothing.

Alternatives. In the event you accept everything as written above, I will stay under the same roof with you like father and daughter for the next few weeks until I move into my own place. In the opposite case, I will be moving out in just one day, and I will take along only what is mine. To everyone else, everything will look normal, as before. I will consider you my father anyway, one way or another. I will maintain a civil but distant communication just like you kept with your parents.

If you do not desire this, I respect your wish and we will not talk from here on, nor will we see each other ever again. If you change your mind, you can let me know and we'll discuss it at that time. If you want to meet Colt, you just let me know.

I will need a response to this letter in the next twenty-four hours. I have nothing else to add. I hope God keeps you in his care.

Your daughter,

Luissa

"I will not agree to your conditions," he said. This was the response I knew would come.

"Then I will move out tomorrow."

He said nothing. His rage had subsided. Or perhaps it was growing. I couldn't be sure—but I didn't have energy for him that night. I walked away from him then, feeling powerful. Seen. In control of my life and my destiny.

The next morning, I left early to go and finalize the contract for the apartment. It was unoccupied, but I had to wait until the following Tuesday for it to be fully cleaned and ready. With my mom's generous gift, plus *my own* salary that I'd finally been able to deposit into *my own* bank account, I was able to afford *my own* apartment. Mine, all mine. It felt surreal.

While sitting in the leasing office, my father called me three times on the office phone, asking me to change my mind and stay with him.

"I'm not changing my mind," I said.

Over the next few days, I did everything to avoid my father, leaving early and returning late, meeting up with Kim and spending time with Colt.

The last night, I worked until nine-thirty. Colt met me at work so we could grab a bite at a restaurant nearby. We shared a plate of shrimp; he ordered a Pepsi and I ordered a pineapple juice, and we talked for hours. Finally, just before one o'clock in the morning, I drove home.

When I walked into the apartment, I immediately smelled tobacco smoke and saw my father waiting, pacing back and forth. Dinner was set at the table with candles. Half a pack of cigarettes sat on the coffee table, alongside a half-dozen butts in an ashtray. I knew he'd smoked when he was young but I had never seen him do so as an adult.

"What is going on?" I asked in Romanian. "What exactly do you want?"

"I called your mother," he replied. "And I recorded the conversation."

I felt chills creep down my arm. My mom? Why was he involving her?

"This is too much for me," I said. He ignored me and started playing the conversation.

As the audio played, I heard the enormity of the lies he told my mom: that I was out of control, bar clubbing every night with different men, drinking, and using drugs with my whore friends from work. The more I heard, the angrier I became. It dawned on me how much I abhorred this man, deep to my core.

"Turn it off," I said.

He just looked at me, a sly smile on his face as I listened to my mother's upset voice on the other line.

"Turn it off!" I yelled.

My volume surprised him, and he slammed the button on the recorder and spun toward me, his face manic. He took his belt off his pants and lifted it in the air, walking toward me to hit me.

I did not move. Nor cower. Instead I looked right at him and said, "You know, I am not afraid of you. If you hit me, I will call the police."

He had hit me once, years earlier. I didn't tolerate it then and I wouldn't tolerate it now. Not that day, not ever again—in any way. He had no right to lay his hands on me. My body was mine. It always had been, now reclaimed from the prison he had built through ever present manipulation and control.

My threat didn't stop him, and he stepped toward me again, the belt lifted to hit me. I stepped to the side and reached for the phone, swiftly dialing 9-1-1. When the operator came on, I quickly told her my address and that my father was not allowing me to leave and to please hurry. My father stared as I spoke, and when I hung up, it struck me that I'd just done the thing I hadn't been able to do in the nearly seven years living under the same roof. I'd finally called the police on my last day with him.

With the knowledge that the police were on their way, my father's violent rage seemed to slump. He was still livid but I didn't think he would hurt me. I calmed down too.

A police officer arrived several minutes later and spoke with both of us. When I said I didn't want to press charges, the officer walked to stand directly in front of my father, who straightened his posture to meet the officer's eyes.

"She is an adult," the policeman said. "You can't force her to stay here."

After the policeman left, I called my mom. I didn't mention the altercation with my father but instead shared my plans to move out. Our conversation was brief. I wanted to hear her voice and let her know I wouldn't be at my father's place anymore. Immediately after we hung up, I went to bed and blocked the door with a chair propped under the handle.

As I lay there awake that night, I thought of my mom. How foolish of my father to try to turn my dear mom against me, to involve her in his evil. He had no right to come between my mother and me, especially after he had stolen so many years of her life.

I woke up at seven-thirty the next morning, dressed, and started packing. Before noon, I was finished, with nearly everything loaded into my car. I didn't have a lot: clothes, a chair, some plates, books, a small TV, some documents. I would return with a truck in a few days to get my desk. I had to be at work at three o'clock that day and still needed to unload at my new apartment.

Before I loaded my last box, I begged my father to let me have my dear Suzette, my little friend and companion during my many years of misery. He refused.

As I carried my last box out of the apartment, he sat on a low wooden stool on the floor, with his elbows on his knees and head in his hands. He looked pitiful and old, a broken man.

When I walked by him, he looked up and gently grabbed my arm.

"Luissa, how could you?" he said. "You must hate me."

"I don't hate you, Father," I replied. My voice was cold. Detached. "I simply don't feel anything anymore when it comes to you." I stopped in front of him and looked down at him, looking him squarely in the eyes. "At first, I felt pain, then hate, then disgust, and finally just a void. One thing is for sure, if I were to see you lying in the middle of the street, I would pass by you and not even wince. You are *nothing* to me."

I walked out the front door and to my car. I drove away that day, heading to my new apartment, and into my new life.

SECTION III

THIRD LIFE IN AMERICA (REBIRTH)

"The greatest sources of our suffering are the lies we tell ourselves."
—Bessel A. van der Kolk, M.D., *The Body Keeps the Score*

10

THE THANKSGIVING WALK

hugged my white rabbit fur jacket close as I kept pace with my mom, strolling past the buildings of Saint Anselm's College, the Abbey Church just ahead. I'd always loved the campus, with its ample trees and lush lawns, and often walked by the church to have a moment with God, even though I had lost touch with my Catholic roots during my years in America.

Today, the campus was not green and bright. It was gray and overcast, enveloped by winter, the crisp near-snow air biting my nose and ears. It was my first Thanksgiving Day as an American citizen, and as I listened to my mom chatter about the feast we'd prepared together and enjoyed that day, I felt grateful. My mom was visiting for the first time since I'd moved to America. She had been there for a few weeks already, staying in my apartment in Nashua, New Hampshire, and would stay until early January. So far, between work shifts, I'd taken her to see various sights nearby: Boston, Concord, Hampton Beach, Portsmouth, and Plymouth, the original settlement by colonists in the United States. She enjoyed everything, but most of all she loved that we were together again.

After my years of isolation, spending this extended time with my mom was heaven. We sat at the table each morning, drinking coffee together and talking about the day ahead. I made tea at night and took in every detail of her face: the lines that had deepened since I'd left, the questions behind her blue eyes, the love in her expression, the way all I had to do was think I needed something—a tomato for dinner, a trash bag, my shoes—and she'd hop up and rush to get it for me.

She was making up for lost time. I was reorienting to normal and soaking in her love.

I'd tried my hand at a traditional Thanksgiving meal that afternoon: mashed potatoes, turkey, stuffing, corn, green beans, and apple pie for dessert. Giving thanks and gratitude together, each in our own way, my mom, Colt, and I had eaten the meal in my little kitchen, dishes piled next to the sink, a candle lit. Afterward, my mom and I had washed dishes together, chatting about family and what they might be doing that day. She talked about Grandma, Aunt Tutti, Uncle Sandu, and Dragoş. I asked about Bîzu and about my friends and colleagues from school and the neighborhood. We shared memories and updates about Padre and relatives. The years that had left their mark on me had passed for everyone else as well; no one was spared by the stamp of time. She told me more about what life was like in Romania now, and how things were better, and asked if I'd ever come back to live there. We both knew the answer. I was an American citizen now. And for better or worse, I had built a life here. I could never go back to my old life, not really.

As we continued our walk through campus, my mom now talking about our plans the next day, I thought about the one tense moment of her visit. We'd had dinner one night with Colt, his parents . . . and my father. As we sat at the restaurant table that evening, I chided myself for inviting him. Why had I asked him to come? In truth, I wanted us all to be together, facing each other, in defiance of what he had professed years ago: "As long as I live, your mother will never come here."

Forgive but never forget. I admit: That's me.

We all met at The Yard restaurant and, after Colt and his parents left, my father and mom argued. It was a circular disagreement, my mom blaming my father for the interruption of my life; my father blaming me for being ungrateful and selfish. At the end of their argument, he asked my mom to remarry him. His offer was as pitiful as he was: He had stage three Parkinson's and needed someone to care for him. An old man whose only motive was locking in a caretaker.

My mom's face registered shock at this offer. Once she composed herself, she said to him, "You repulse me. Even if we were the only two people on the planet, I would never marry you."

As he stood to leave that evening, he glared at me and said, "Why did you take me to this distasteful place?"

He left that day, alone, except for his demons.

Now, walking through Saint Anselm's on Thanksgiving Day, my mom's stream of conversation had fallen to silence. The campus was empty—we hadn't seen anyone for at least half an hour. Thanksgiving mass must have ended hours earlier because the church was closed up tight. Maybe the monks were inside enjoying a Thanksgiving dinner of their own.

As we walked past the steps of the Abbey, I heard my mom's footsteps stop. I turned, wondering what she'd seen that caught her interest. I had always loved the quaint chapel—the bricks, the doors, the trees surrounding its façade. But my mom wasn't looking at the church; she was looking at me.

"*Și școala ta?*" she said. And your school?

I felt goosebumps rise on my neck. A moment earlier, I'd been enjoying the winter afternoon and chatting lightly about what we'd do the next day. Now I felt like she'd shined a spotlight on my failings.

"What about school?" I said.

I knew what she meant. While my intentions had been to enroll in school the previous fall semester, life had gotten in the way. I was barely staying afloat financially with my three jobs. I was in a relationship that was beginning to show its edges, no longer light and exciting like it once was. I was healing from unspeakable trauma and hadn't told a soul about what I'd really gone through. It felt like life kept going, going, going, but I wasn't living. I was suffering, but I was trying hard to do so with a smile.

School . . . my dream that had gotten me into this predicament felt more and more like a *Fata Morgana*, a mirage in the desert. Soon it would be eight years since I'd arrived in America. I was almost twenty-seven years old with a bachelor's degree still in the works, not yet enrolled in medical school. Where had the time gone?

Colt . . . the truth, as I learned later on, is that I should not have jumped into a relationship in an attempt to heal myself. I was vulnerable. I needed someone to love me unconditionally and to love back. I was like a hurt creature looking for anything that was better than what I had suffered through. Colt was a refuge. But despite making good money as an electrician, I soon discovered that Colt had some major issues: He gambled a lot, drank when he lost, and when he won, he drank more—only to lose again. Plus, he was unfaithful. In the beginning, I thought my support and our love would change him. But as I would eventually learn, no one can change someone else. They can only change themselves.

Still, I told myself, there was a lot of good around me. I was living my life now as an independent, bright young woman with so much potential. I had what anyone would dream of: financial independence, liberty to speak freely, and freedom to act on my own free will, love, pray, and *live*. I now had the capability to break past who I had been allowed to be and step fully into who I was destined to become. The foundation of my life had been laid, cemented with my tears, pain, and hope. It was time to build my life. What more could I want?

But I was hiding deep scars and oozing wounds, and my soul was grieving. I was unfulfilled. Sometimes, I would look at myself in the mirror and see what no one else was allowed to: the truth of my pain. Who was this person I saw in the reflection? I would see my true self just for a moment and then quickly cover my pain with my jovial, optimistic self. I'd walk out into the world again, busy living but never forgetting.

"What are your plans?" Mom finally said, interrupting my thoughts. "Are you going to finish what you set out to do?"

"I don't know, Mom," I said. "I don't know if it's ever going to happen."

I tugged my coat around my body as though it were protective armor.

How could I explain to her that my dream was slipping away, just like the last nearly eight years of my life?

"You see how much I work, Mom. I just can't see it happening anymore."

This was the first time I'd admitted this out loud: that I wasn't sure if I would graduate from college, let alone achieve my lifelong goal of becoming a doctor. That maybe I wasn't cut out for the dream that had kept me alive and sane while I suffered my father's abuse; that maybe I was destined for a different life, one of a real estate saleswoman or a secretary or a grocer . . . one of the many jobs I'd already held. I knew there was no shame in that work, and that I made an honest salary, and that I was in a country so many would be grateful to live in. But the ache of my dream sat in the pit of my stomach. Like coal smoldering with a spark that's about to die. The dream was still deep inside me, but it was almost gone. I'd almost let it go.

My mom's eyes met mine, holding my gaze, the gloom and cold around us seeping deep within me as I thought: How can I let this woman down? After all I've suffered, all she's suffered, how can I disappoint her?

We continued walking, my mind running like I'd ingested adrenaline. I had no savings. I was struggling just to pay my $535 per month rent, utilities, insurance, car payment, groceries, and everyday life expenses.

All those years. All those years with my father, the one thing that had kept me going was my dream. It became almost like an obsession. During the sexual assaults, the emotional abuse, the financial control, the mind games—I'd pushed through all of it because I believed in myself and my destiny to become a doctor. Soon after I arrived in America, this dream became my lifeline. I hung on to it tightly, like my life depended on it, because it did. When all seemed lost, this idea became an idol; when all else failed, this vision was the thin straw I grabbed on to. I would have drowned otherwise—I know I would have. Likely, I would have become a monster like him, full of sorrow, despair, and bitterness. But Christ showed His love for me through my memories of childhood, my mother's ongoing love, my dream, and my furry blue-eyed companion.

But now? I felt too broken, too burdened, too broke. It felt impossible to find a way to pay for college, and then medical school, let alone make time for classes amid the schedule of multiple jobs I kept just to pay the bills.

I'd almost let my dream go. Almost.

Or perhaps I needed this break in time to pause, recollect, and reorient. Instead of my dream being a lifeline in the face of despair, would I now feel the natural impulse to finish what I started in the summer of 1986, the year I started preparing to retake the admission test in Romania?

My mom said nothing more that afternoon. She never pushed me, never questioned why I hadn't already started classes, never told me not to give up. But she didn't have to. I understood what she meant by her questions: Luissa, I believe in you.

While we didn't talk about school again that day or during the rest of her visit, her questions rolled over and over in my mind: What about your school? Are you going to finish?

Was I going to finish what I'd started? Was I going to reach the finish line? Was I going to become a doctor? Was all of this suffering going to have a happy ending? Not just an acceptable outcome but a meaningful one? An achievement that might release me from my pain?

The time had come to change the lens I was looking at life through. I needed to let go of the past.

Mom left for Romania in January as planned. Within a couple of weeks, I called the University of Massachusetts in Lowell and started the application process. A few weeks later, I was admitted to pursue my bachelor's in biology. When the school tried to only transfer fourteen credits for the fifty-plus on my transcripts, I went from department head to department head and pleaded for them to look at my transcripts again. I was a woman on a mission, and the fire my mom had relit wasn't going to be put out so easily. I couldn't redo all those past years of school.

Eventually, I was able to transfer 41 credits, giving me solid footing toward the 121 I would need to graduate. As a "returning adult" at the age of twenty-seven, I was also now considered independent from my family and could file the Free Application for Federal Student Aid (FAFSA) independently, which I knew meant I should receive a full scholarship for at least the first year through the US government. It started to feel like the dominoes were finally stacked in my favor. The first few were heavy—I had to struggle to topple them one at a time—but eventually they would catch and fall one by one, directly toward my dream.

Combined with minimal loans to keep me afloat, I was able to support myself by cutting down my work hours to weekends. Market Basket paid time and a half on Sundays, so as front-end assistant manager I would work open to close, or as I liked to call it, "7A to 7P." It was more like eight o'clock because the store had to be completely tidied up and the front end of the store had to be cleaned and restocked. I used to say to myself half-seriously, half-joking: "People come, people go, and I am still here." No wonder I have an aversion to grocery stores to this day!

But no matter what I had to do to pay the bills, there was not going to be any more classes here and there; no more picking away at my dream. I planned to take eighteen to twenty credit hours a semester plus summer classes so I could finish in two years. There was no negotiation.

My mom had rekindled my fire, and I was back. Nothing could stop me now. I would become a doctor no matter what.

—

The first semester was rough. Getting back into the routine and discipline, attending classes back-to-back, spending long hours studying, keeping up with the pace of the eighteen-year-olds around me—it was overwhelming. I failed my first biochemistry exam, which was the wake-up call I needed to get help. I started going to my teacher every Thursday and began to relearn studying and exam-taking techniques. By the end of that semester, I managed to pull through with a B minus in that class.

Slowly, over the years of my bachelor's, everything started coming together. Every semester, my grades were higher and my GPA improved. I made the dean's list both semesters of my final year.

And then, I did it: After all those years, I finally finished my bachelor's magna cum laude. But as with most things in my life to that point, I didn't pause long to celebrate. There were no graduation announcements sent out; there was no party or celebration dinner. There was, however, something even more special: I brought my mom and my grandmother to America for my graduation. They had to be there with me. My success was their success. I was ecstatic. I felt victorious. The light was shining slightly brighter on the horizon.

After graduation, I got right back to working toward my dream. During the summer of 1997, I enrolled in the Kaplan MCAT review course, and twice per week for five weeks I would walk from the research center in Boston I now worked at, to the Kaplan Center for my three-hour class, then drive back home.

As I prepared to take the MCAT, I started analyzing my odds toward the next milestone: enrolling in medical school. Even with my strong grades, I knew my limited experience in the medical field and my age, now twenty-nine, made me less competitive against other applicants. With my dream still burning within me, I took a gap year to work in the research lab at the GRASP Center—Gastroenterology Research on Absorptive and Secretory Processes Center, which was part of Tufts Medical Center—researching gastrointestinal strains. While the job only paid $10 per hour, it was also an intentional résumé builder that I had known would help set me apart from other medical school candidates. Getting this job had felt like I was "grabbing God by the foot," as they say in Romania. It was another domino in my favor.

But it didn't make my schedule easy. I was now living in Londonderry and the drive to my new workplace was forty-five miles one way into Boston. Every day. Then after my work shift at the lab ended at three o'clock each afternoon, I had another shift as a counselor each evening from five to eleven o'clock at Pathfinders, a state-run organization for mentally ill homeless people.

While working at Pathfinders, I met another counselor, Eduard, who was introduced to me by my friend—his sister, Bea. He was ten years younger than me, born and raised in Kenya in a family of four kids. He had a strong build, a calm demeanor, and when he spoke his boyish face often lit up in a shy, candid smile. He was interested in me, but I turned away his advances at first. Having just gotten out of a relationship, I'd sworn off men. And anyway, I had more serious matters to focus on, namely medical school.

But Eduard was persistent. And kind. One evening, Bea and I went out dancing after work, leaving my car in front of Pathfinders and both riding in hers. When we returned at around one in the morning, there was Eduard, waiting by my parked car to make sure we made it back safely. I said a quick "hi!" and "thanks," then got in my car and drove home. But I didn't forget his gesture. Nobody had ever done anything like that for me before. Over time, we began dating. As our relationship progressed, I continued to devote myself to my studies and work.

In addition to my job in the lab and at Pathfinders, on weekends I would do translation work for a local language business, which paid well at $24.00 per hour, an amount I had never earned before. If I could get an interpreting job here and there, I would use a vacation day at my other jobs and make extra money. I couldn't afford to go on vacations anyway.

While this schedule was favorable for my résumé and bank account, I only lasted three months making the daily commute in my car. I was sleep deprived and driving became unsafe. One afternoon, while driving home after work, I noticed I started to fall asleep at the wheel. I knew something had to change so I could get enough sleep—and not put myself and others in danger.

Then I found a bus station that was a five-minute drive from my apartment, with a bus into Boston each morning, so I decided that was the way to go if I didn't want to kill myself or someone else.

Each early morning, I parked my car at the station and boarded the bus at six o'clock to head into the city. Once inside the warm bus, I would fold my jacket into a pillow, hug my satchel to my chest, and fall asleep. When the bus made its last stop, I'd wake abruptly, sitting up and rubbing my palms over my cheeks to wake myself up. Then I'd gather my jacket and satchel, which usually held my lunch, a textbook to study at lunch, and some papers I needed to bring back to the lab. Each late afternoon, I'd cocoon myself in the second or third row of the bus, with my jacket as a pillow, and sleep until the line ended, then drive the short distance home. With the fifty-minute naps each way, I was getting enough broken sleep to not feel like a zombie anymore.

Now several weeks into my routine, I was no longer sheepish about sleeping. The driver knew by now that I survived through these commutes. Without my daily bus nap to and from work, I didn't know how I'd function as I kept moving toward my goal.

During the summer over a period of two months, I had sent out about seventy applications, all mailed by hand, and now all I could do was wait to hear if I would be able to realize my dream. I knew I could excel in medical school, but one looming fear remained: What if I didn't get in?

Then, on January 15, 1998, I received a letter that finally dissolved this long-held fear. I received an acceptance letter from the University of New England College of Osteopathic Medicine.

As I read the words, I breathed a bone-deep sigh of relief.

Yes. After everything, I would be a doctor.

This meant everything to me.

One week later, a second acceptance letter, this time from Midwestern University, arrived and this felt incredible too—like an affirmation, to myself and the world, that my getting into medical school was not an accident. Soon, I had received a third, fourth, and fifth acceptance. All of these were meaningful to me, further validation of my work and belonging on this path: I got into five medical schools and knew that couldn't possibly be an accident. It just couldn't.

Doors were opening—and now I hoped one more would as well. A scholarship with the Air Force.

One morning, as I stepped off the bus into the crisp late-winter air, I wondered if today would be the day I'd hear from them. I gave the driver a little wave, wishing him a good day, and began walking.

I'd been waiting for weeks to hear about the military Health Profession Scholarship Program, or the HPSP. Getting my medical education paid by the military through a payback commitment sounded like a dream to me. To qualify, I needed to be an American citizen, have a clean record, be in good health, have an undergraduate degree with an excellent GPA, be younger than thirty-six, and be willing to serve my country and honor the payback commitment. Check and check for the entire qualification list. I had called the Navy recruiting center but hadn't gotten a reply. When I called the Air Force, though, I heard back the next day from the recruiter, Staff Sergeant Wallace, and began my journey with the US Air Force.

Getting into school was a required step to be eligible for the scholarship, but winning the funding was highly competitive. I also knew my application wasn't as strong as I'd like it to be. While I had a decent MCAT score, it wasn't as high as I had wished, and I knew it could be a gatekeeper to receiving the money I needed to pay for college. Still, five medical schools had said "yes" to me after the usual in-person visits and interviews—wouldn't the Air Force too?

That thought nearly stopped my steps. I slowed, repeating the words in my head: Five medical schools had said "yes." I was in. So close to the dream I'd almost let slip away, the one that kept me going those many years with my father, the theme of my life since fifth grade: my destiny to become a doctor.

As I waited at the crosswalk to the research center, I thought back over the past three years. My now-over relationship with Colt gave me the experience of having a boyfriend, and the normalcy of our relationship was a launchpad for freedom. Experiencing a typical dating life and romantic love—even though it didn't last—was an entry point into a new life.

I thought, too, of the years pursuing my bachelor's, working multiple jobs and taking out minimal loans to survive. The daily "lunches" in the student building, covertly grabbing handfuls of saltine crackers and little plastic tubs of peanut butter and jelly from the salad bar and finding a far-off corner in which to eat them, laying out a napkin as a plate and using a plastic knife to spread the peanut butter on the crackers. The inner work I'd done, not with a therapist but within my own mind, to breathe through the flashbacks and avoid reliving the past, instead focusing on rebuilding my present and reaching a future I was proud of. Studying for the MCAT: the classes I took, the nights hovering over the study materials, my eyelids drooping while I pushed myself to keep going for another fifteen minutes. The applications to medical school, which cost a small fortune, and the feeling when acceptance after acceptance rolled in, validation that I was worthy of the dream I almost abandoned.

Deep inside I had learned to conquer my self-doubts, the voice inside that told me I was not good enough to become a doctor. As my father used to tell me during our arguments, "Luissa, take it from me, you will *never* get anywhere. You are a nobody without me."

But he was wrong.

So much had happened in the past few years: endless work, studying, my relationship with Colt. And so much was ahead of me: medical school, residency, finally becoming the doctor I knew I was destined to become.

But there was also the question of money. Being accepted into medical school was one thing, but I still had to find the money to pay the tuition.

This scholarship could solve that problem.

As I entered the lab building, I thought of my last meeting with SSgt Wallace. His words echoed through my brain like a cough in an empty auditorium: "Your file is very strong. If the Air Force can get over the fact that your MCATs are the lowest part of your entire file, which I believe they will—if they look at you as a whole person, you'll get it. If they look at it just from the numbers, you won't."

I had the grades, the passion, the smarts. I'd graduated magna cum laude, was working as a researcher, and had a multifaceted background that set me apart from other candidates. I had a sparkling recommendation from my mentor, Dr. Levine. I even had the five medical school acceptance letters, of which I'd chosen the University of New England College of Osteopathic Medicine in Maine. What I didn't have was the funding to attend. If I received the Air Force scholarship, they would pay my entire medical school tuition, books, fees—everything—and give me $960 per month to live on, which felt like a fortune.

Sliding into my desk chair, I tucked my satchel underneath my desk and looked expectantly at the phone. It was only 7:01. Surely he wouldn't be calling this early, I thought. Might as well get started on work to keep my mind occupied. I went into the lab, reviewed the long list of experiments to be done that day, and started prepping the gels for the petri dishes. My mind soon became preoccupied by the task at hand.

He didn't call that morning. Or during lunch, which I ate at my desk next to my phone. By two o'clock, I started to worry. Would he call me if it was a no or just send a letter? He should have called at least a day ago. What was going on?

While I tried to focus on my work that afternoon, I was distracted. Nausea began to grow. I drank nearly an entire bottle of water to settle my stomach. As I wrapped up my findings from that morning and wrote them in the logbook, I couldn't help glancing at the clock every few minutes.

The minutes creeped by slowly.

One by one.

By three-thirty, I was almost in a panic. I had missed my normal bus, but I didn't care. I would just take the next one.

Then the main line to the lab rang. I grabbed the receiver on my desk before the first ring ended.

"Hello, GRASP Center, this is Luissa," I said, my standard professional greeting.

"Luissa," a deep voice said on the other end. "This is SSgt Wallace."

"Hello," I said quickly. "How are you?"

"I'm fine, I'm fine. Look, I wanted to tell you this over the phone—"

"Yes?"

"Luissa, you did it. You got a scholarship."

My hand holding the receiver began to tingle. I breathed in deeply, a sensation of disbelief and relief flooding my lungs, veins, muscles—my entire body. A smile swept across my face and tears spilled down my cheeks. I wiped them quickly, not wanting my coworkers to see.

"I did it," I echoed. "I'm going to become a doctor."

"That's right, kid. You're in. Come to my office at 0800 tomorrow morning and let's sign you on."

I hung up that afternoon a new woman. A woman yet again reborn. A woman who had not yet become a doctor but who had the keys in her hand to her greatest dreams. I felt like I had finally released my nineteen-year-old self from the chains of decisions that weren't hers, from the trauma she endured for nearly seven years, from the pain of losing her family and country, from the loss she'd felt from being stripped of her identity so many years back. I set her free. I blessed and released her suffering, and while I was not healed, I knew I was on the path to healing myself while I healed others as a physician.

This was it! My dream come true!

I knew I still had another four years of medical school and a few more years of residency after that. I would be in my mid-thirties by the time I ended my medical training. I had lost so much time. But I knew focusing on the loss wouldn't propel me forward. I had to keep going. For Old Luissa, for New Luissa, and now for Reborn Luissa.

I wish I could say that afternoon healed me completely. The truth is that would take decades, and I am still on that path. But that afternoon, sitting at my desk, the weight of the phone still in my palms, I felt like I had a fighting chance.

The next morning, I arrived at the Air Force recruiting center, where SSgt Wallace was waiting for me. I sat across from Captain Marcus, who was in her forties with short, light brown hair, blue eyes, and thin-rimmed glasses, and was dressed in the Air Force blues attire. SSgt Wallace sat just behind me. Captain Marcus was set to interview me and give the final blessing; SSgt Wallace would swear me in.

After a brief introduction about the scope of our visit, Captain Marcus smiled warmly at me and asked, "Which school of the five you got letters from is your first choice, Luissa?"

"University of New England, ma'am," I said.

She looked briefly down at the list, then back at me. "And why is that?"

My answer came out quickly: "Because I am from here, from New England, ma'am."

She smiled. "You made a good choice. I approve."

SSgt Wallace spoke from behind me. "Are you ready to take the oath?"

"Yes, sir."

My heart sat high in my throat as I took the oath.

"Congratulations, my dear," Captain Marcus said and shook my hand. "Welcome to the United States Air Force!"

And for the second time since April 18, 1987, I knew that America had my back. The first time was on December 3, 1993, when I became one of its citizens. The second time was that day, March 9, 1998.

I felt proud. I felt worthy. I felt unstoppable.

11

BECOMING

Over the next days, weeks, and years of medical school, I was constantly in motion. Busy building toward my dream—brick by brick, layer of mortar in between—slowly but surely advancing, making up for the seven-plus years I'd lost. I felt like I had something to prove, not to my peers, teachers, or patients, but to myself. I had fought hard and suffered greatly; this, I knew, was the near-final inning that just happened to stretch across four years. Medical school challenged me, but I had prepared myself for its rigor. Residency would follow. Maybe after all the pushing, I could fully breathe, deeply exhale. I could finally stop being afraid something would happen and keep me from achieving this dream.

Rest. Ease. Contentment. What would that be like?

It felt like I was completing the final miles of a full-length 26.2-mile marathon race, fighting like hell to finally achieve my dream, always with my eyes on the goal. It didn't matter that I was exhausted. Nothing would stand in my way of completing medical school.

The first two years of medical school are only classes, meant to lay the foundation of medical knowledge; the following two years are clinical rotations, where we learn to evaluate and treat real patients. To get as much studying and skills practice in as possible, I put together a schedule each term that included short naps between classes. While taking classes, I practically moved into the school library, spending hours poring over my medical books as I handwrote notes, taking naps in one of the study rooms to refresh myself for the next class or block of studying. I spent my evenings in the cadaver skills lab alongside my classmates, hovering over donated bodies to learn the muscles, organs, and bones in preparation for an upcoming test. Between classes, I would often sit in one of the large windows in the hallway and eat quickly, then lay my head down on a thick textbook and sleep. One term, I had it down to an exact science: nine minutes to eat, eleven minutes to sleep. A quick cat nap, then off to my next round of classes.

But even though I was heads-down, I wasn't lonely. I had strong relationships, something I hadn't enjoyed during those years with my father. I had my boyfriend, Eduard, who had changed jobs and moved to a nearby town when I started medical school. When I was in his presence, I felt I could relax, let my guard down and rest awhile. I could finally recharge my batteries from maintaining my constant vigilance. We were opposites who were drawn to each other, and that was a good thing—I certainly didn't need another type A person around me.

I also had made several friends in my program. A couple of my classmates rented a house together by the beach, and we would sit around a table in the back under a big umbrella and study, usually four or five of us together.

Still, even with these positive relationships, I didn't feel like I could slow down to enjoy my life. Not only did I feel behind in my career, but my biological clock was ticking too. Having children was part of my dream life, and yet I knew my limits. The idea of caring for a baby during med school was frightening. One of my classmates had gotten pregnant and had to take the year off after she had the baby. Med school is taxing on its own and I knew I didn't need any added stress. Eduard and I had become serious and discussed having a family someday; we agreed that the best thing would be to wait. So I remained focused on one part of my dream—the rest would have to come later.

Each time I passed a skills test, aced an exam, or finished a course, it was like I was checking a box. There was no celebration. No recognition of the small achievements on the marathon to my big goal. While I was making progress, I always felt behind. Plus, I constantly reminded myself, graduating medical school was only the start. I still had to match with a residency program.

I was so focused, I never lifted my head up long enough to realize I was walking straight into my dream. I was waiting to exhale, afraid to stop and take a breath, because I worried this beautiful dream would dissipate into another cruel mishap.

A person can only understand this mental state if one experiences trauma, especially during childhood or early adulthood while the brain is at different stages of immaturity. When the brain is deprived of love or safety, it's like growing up always hungry and in scarcity. Hopefully, at some point in adulthood, a survivor will finally have plenty of resources—however, they will continue to overreach and hoard because they have been wired by scarcity and do not want to experience that lack again. Hypervigilance becomes homeostasis.

But I wasn't threatened or deprived anymore. I was free. And so, while this professional dream of mine was no longer an obsession that kept me alive, I remained hypervigilant about staying on course. Eyes on the prize . . . always. It was the same with my financial stability—it equaled independence.

While I was focused, I also felt powerful. I was choosing my destiny. I was following my dream. I had hope for a beautiful life and I would do anything to make it a reality.

After my second year, it was time for my clinical rotations. I had both core rotations, which were mandatory core clinical classes for completing medical school, and selectives, which were preset rotations for medical specialties outside the scope of the core classes. Rotations were our opportunity to try different specialties and see what stuck. Like most osteopathic schools at the time in the United States, my school didn't have a hospital on or near campus, therefore we had our rotation tracks contracted with hospitals in several locations: Newark, New Jersey; Albany, New York; Columbus, Ohio; upstate Maine; and Lehigh Valley, Pennsylvania. My placement, chosen by a lottery system, was at St. Joseph's Hospital in Newark, New Jersey, and my track started with general surgery.

I thought being a general surgeon would be a perfect fit, but I soon realized it wasn't for me. The patient-doctor connection was not at all what I expected. A lot of surgery, not enough continuity of care. To make matters worse, the surgery clerkship director, an old Indian physician, concluded the exit interview by saying, "Student doctor, I don't think you would make a good surgeon. You are just too strong for a woman."

I was aghast. I wanted to reply, "How should I be, then? More subservient?"

Instead, I swallowed my words, said a brief "thanks," and walked out.

My next rotation was obstetrics and gynecology, and I loved it! It had the right mix of continuous patient care and procedures, all devoted to women's health. Obstetrics was the happy journey of pregnancy, the miracle of bringing a baby into the world, fulfilling a family's wish, and creating a complete unit. Gynecology was caring for women of all stages of life, performing surgeries, providing counseling, and offering support, treatment, and a better quality of life.

Adding to that was my own experience as a young woman, both from communism and from my first years here in America. I deeply believe that every woman should have full autonomy over her own body and be free to make her own decision about whether the time is right to bring another life into this world to love, cherish, and provide for. In Romania, I had lost two family friends to illegal abortions. The basic freedom to terminate a pregnancy was censored and punished by communism. In America, I had my own misfortunes due to the repeated sexual abuse. What would I have become if I hadn't had the right to choose? What kind of life would those offspring have?

I knew I wanted to help women through joy and hard choices, wellness and sickness, hope and fear. And to do so with more than nonjudgment—with true care and understanding.

So I made my decision: I would pursue becoming an OB-GYN.

As part of the Health Profession Scholarship with the Air Force, I was also required to spend four weeks each summer in various medical rotations at Air Force bases. While this schedule didn't enable me to rest between medical school years, I gained extra experience and was paid for six full weeks of active-duty work, even though I only worked four. Combined with the small monthly stipend during the school year, these earnings allowed me to go through medical school without taking another job. During my third Air Force summer military assignment, I rotated at Lackland Air Force Base in San Antonio and fell in love with the city and its people. I wanted nothing more than to complete residency at the base there.

The last miles of my marathon were unfolding before me. I needed to complete this stage, medical school, and then I'd be nearly done with the race. Each mile brought me closer to my dream and further away from the life I had left behind with my father. Closer to normal, further from pain. Closer to becoming a doctor. To healing myself and others.

—

While in school, my relationship with my boyfriend, Eduard, continued to deepen. We moved in together during the summer of my second year of med school, into a one-bedroom apartment about three miles from school.

Before we moved in together, I had opened my heart to him. It was the first time I'd told anyone the truth of what happened to me. My words were a lot to take in: such a painful story, bordering on the unreal. After all, who does that to someone, let alone their child? We cried together. He wanted to meet my father to confront him, to make him suffer. But I said to him: "There is no use. The past is in the past. I forgave him so the resentment would not continue to poison me. I let go to be able to live in the present, start healing, and look forward to the future. You must too. He is getting what he deserves. He is alone. He will die alone."

There is a God, I thought. *This is justice.*

Eduard made me feel safe and seen. I had trusted him with my secret and his response had been love. Our relationship became even stronger that day.

The biggest challenge we faced was time. In the pockets I found between classes and rotations, we would often share picnic meals on the floor of our living room. I'd bring home food from the cafeteria and we'd sit and talk for the bit of time we had, before one of us would need to head off—him to a work shift at Home Depot or me to a study session.

The normalcy of our relationship felt right. Good. I still felt behind, but it seemed like I was finally catching up. I was partway through medical school, with a boyfriend I loved. I had friends. I was respected by my teachers and peers.

During my second year of medical school, Eduard drove me to Fox Hill, his favorite spot in the small town of Billerica, Massachusetts. He took me on a walk that morning to the top of a secluded hill. When we got to the top, he kneeled and said softly, "Will you marry me?"

"Yes!" I replied, tears flowing down my cheeks, bewildered that this was truly happening.

It was my birthday. Eduard had marked anew a day that had been stolen from me all those years ago. I could never have believed, not in a million years, that I would experience anything remotely normal in my life ever again. And here it was. A normal relationship. A normal young man asking me to marry him.

We were in love with each other. How much more normal could it get than that?

Our wedding was on a cold, sunny January day in Biddeford, Maine. It was a simple church wedding, with a couple of school friends—Catrina and her friend Mark; Kate, my schoolmate, as maid of honor; and Dave, her husband, as best man—my anatomy professor as our professional photographer, and the priest, who forgot our wedding day, showing up late. Unfortunately, Kim, whom I had maintained a close friendship with over the years, wasn't able to make it.

Neither of us told our families about the wedding until afterwards. I wore a simple white dress with a high-cut neckline and plunging back that I bought for $100, paired with white satin shoes. Catrina wove freesia into my hair. From the town's small patisserie we bought a little cake with two hearts, one white chocolate and one dark chocolate. I carried a modest bouquet, white freesias and roses. We were poor and didn't have the means to host a fancy wedding ceremony, but it was meaningful and moving.

After the wedding, Eduard and I had lunch together at Bugaboo Creek Steakhouse on the way to northern New Hampshire, then spent the honeymoon weekend in a quaint bed and breakfast in the White Mountains, which was just two hours away by car. Eduard and I both believed in the simple beauties in life and enjoyed this celebration with just the two of us. It was simple, beautiful, true love. My wounds were slowly healing.

After our weekend honeymoon, I returned to my rotation that following Monday. Back to the whirlwind of my life. Married now but still me, a little bit closer to normal, in the thick of pursuing my dreams. Pushing, always pushing, to reach the next milestone. Stopping at nothing to become the doctor I knew I was meant to become.

Soon after we married, during my third year of medical school, we moved to Newark, New Jersey, so I could start my clinical rotations at St. Joseph's Hospital. The patients there were mostly poor, many with a host of afflictions, from untreated diabetes to HIV. It was a difficult job because many patients were suffering and some were alone and angry—at life, at themselves, at the system, at anything and everything. Life had been hard for them. But I also saw clearly that many had a choice: to take the medicine we offered or not; to take steps to heal or not. I experienced their despair firsthand. And I could relate: I knew the difference between accepting that you're a victim versus deciding that you're a survivor.

There, I also lost my first patient, Samuel—not because I'd done anything wrong but simply because he was beyond what we could do medically to save him. I used to go see Samuel every day, whether I had him on my patient list or not. He was a quiet man who accepted his chronic diagnosis, systemic sclerosis, and was living his last days in peace.

It happened on a Monday morning. After the early morning rounds with the team I went by to see him, but his bed was made and he was gone. I went back to the nurse's station and asked her about Samuel.

Without looking up from the papers she was analyzing, she replied, "He expired."

"What do you mean, expired?" I asked, confused.

She finally looked up at me. "You know, dead."

I slowly turned around and walked away, still trying to process that word: expired. As in a product that is no longer good, beyond its term, and now must be discarded. It was a fact that the patient was dead, but couldn't we be more caring and less cold? We didn't have to become distant and detached. Patients are fellow humans, after all. In that moment, I promised to myself to never become hardened and to maintain my humanity when caring for patients. The loss stayed with me for days, but I had to carry on, continue learning, and keep practicing the art of medicine if I was going to save lives as a doctor.

As I went through the traditional path to becoming a doctor, I knew I was anything but traditional. While I wasn't the oldest resident—a few had been licensed doctors in foreign countries who had to humble themselves to complete medical school and residency again to practice in the United States—I was older than many of my peers. If I had gone straight from high school, through my bachelor's, medical school, residency, and fellowship, I could have been practicing medicine by age thirty-two as a full-fledged maternal-fetal medicine specialist, which was the path I'd decided on. Instead, I was in my thirties and still had residency ahead of me. Not only did that put me behind in my career but it also impacted my long-term earning potential. I'd never regain those years.

On top of that, I was a foreigner and a woman. If my peers and professors knew my backstory . . . well, I didn't want to find out what would happen. I vowed to myself to keep my secret.

I was tired, but there was no stopping. Never. I would only stop once I made it all the way through, once I had my diploma and my license. As long as I upheld my end of the bargain, which I would, no one could ever take being a doctor away from me. I could not allow myself to become distracted—and honestly, nothing could have distracted me.

This was my last chance. The only opportunity to finish this journey that started just after my nineteenth birthday.

On days when I felt especially tired, I often reflected on my undergrad mentor who wrote one of my letters of recommendation, Dr. Levine. While he wasn't a scientist or physician—he taught literature and human studies—he had been one of my greatest encouragers to achieve my dream. An older, heavyset Jewish gentleman, he played the cello beautifully, was very well read, and was an amazing mentor who sometimes invited me to his office to play chess or to his little house across the Charles River in Cambridge to talk over tea. He believed in me. During these talks, he'd listen for long stretches of time before offering some striking bit of wisdom I'd reflect on for days.

I remember one such day, when I went over to his house after my usual study time to take my mind off books and to talk about the usual: school and goals. I could hear him playing the cello from the driveway, the prelude from Bach's Cello Suite No. 1, an amazing piece that soothed my ears and heart. I never tired of listening to that piece. I entered the front door that he always left unlocked—"I welcome everyone to take all my junk," he would say—and stood there quietly, absorbing the music. He finished the piece, then turned toward me.

"Well, look who snuck in here like a little mouse," he said. "Here, grab a seat and let's visit. Tea?"

I nodded. "Of course. Thank you."

I made myself comfortable on the faded blue fabric chaise, taking in the now-quiet space and the sun's setting rays coming through the window. After a few minutes, he returned, handed me the teacup, and took a seat across from mine. At one point in the conversation, he leaned forward and met my eyes.

"Imagine driving down a highway," he said, "and there are exits along the way, with big signs. One says, 'stop here and have a little bit of fun,' or 'stop here and eat something,' or 'stop here and rest awhile.'"

I nodded, knowing a lesson was coming, but said nothing as he went on.

"It's fine if you get off the highway. Make a short stop, have some nourishment, take a break. But make sure you get back on the highway because you need to get to your destination."

He was right, of course. But as much as I wanted to follow his advice, I felt like I didn't even want to stop to get gas as I traveled toward my dream. I didn't want anything to slow me down. I was on a trajectory to become a doctor. I must get it done. I had lost more than seven years of my life and I couldn't lose a moment more, not for anything.

It wasn't until my final rotations of medical school in the spring of 2002, and after Eduard and I had bought our first house in Springboro, Ohio—a 2,500-square-foot home on a lake, with the down payment borrowed from my close friend, Kim, and a military home loan—that I started to fully believe my dream would come true. I would sit on our back porch, look out on the water, and think about my future. That I would become a doctor. That my life would return to me. That I would reclaim my own destiny.

That I would prove my father wrong.

That I would prove myself right.

—

As I neared the end of medical school, I lined up the next stages of my life. Since I wanted to remain in the military, I only applied to military residency programs, two to be precise. I sighed in relief when I matched with an OB-GYN combined program through Wright-Patterson Medical Center and Wright State University in Dayton, Ohio. Upon completing the four years of residency, I would start my four-year payback commitment to the Air Force.

Happiest of all, I was pregnant and would welcome my son in early September, a couple of months after I started my residency. I had hustled extra hard to finish my rotations a few months before graduation, which was scheduled for June 1st. Eduard and I worked on a few projects around the home and finished the nursery. I signed up for Lamaze classes. I wanted to rest between medical school and residency so I could prepare myself for the arrival of our first baby. Now that I was nearing the end of my second trimester, I needed some downtime. If all went as planned, I would start the OB-GYN residency at the beginning of June, have my son in early September, enjoy the much-cherished bonding time with my baby during my four weeks of maternity leave, and then go on to finish my four years of training in OB-GYN.

—

Eduard and I left for Maine at the beginning of graduation week, the last week of May, to attend my long-awaited ceremony that Saturday. The best part: My mom and grandma would be there. They had flown in from

Romania and were staying with Kim and her husband, Chad, at the beautiful house they'd built in Seabrook, New Hampshire, which was about forty-five minutes from campus.

Eduard and I enjoyed the five days of celebration leading up to medical school graduation. We stayed in the simple dorm on campus the school had provided us graduates so we could be close to the festivities, and we picked up my mom and grandma each day after meals and various social events with my colleagues: golfing, strolling along the nearby beach, dipping in the cold ocean, basking in the hot summer sun. Other than some intermittent lower back discomfort, my underwear being unusually wet, and my belly tightening, life was good. I quickly brushed my symptoms off, blaming it on the sun, the walking, and being as busy as I was, wanting to focus on the fun we were having.

Relief and excitement pulsed through our graduating class. We were all there celebrating this incredible accomplishment together, except for three of us: one woman who had to take a year off due to becoming a mother, and two students who very sadly had passed away due to medical reasons.

The rest of us had made it through. We were almost doctors. All we had to do was walk across that stage and accept our diplomas, and we'd be able to add "Doctor of Osteopathic Medicine" to our titles.

Finally, it was the night before my medical school graduation. The next day, I would put on my cap and gown and walk across the stage to accept my medical school diploma. I knew accepting that piece of paper would feel like I was walking across a threshold to a new life with my young family and future career as an OB-GYN.

The night before the ceremony, Eduard and I stayed at Kim's so we could all travel to campus together for the ceremony. I was twenty-five weeks and four days pregnant and getting into the uncomfortable stage of late-second trimester. Mom, Grandma, Eduard, and I spent a quiet evening with our hosts at their house, sharing stories, laughing, and making plans for the next day. My activities had kept me busy earlier that day and now back pain was coming and going more often. I listened to my body and lay down on the couch, noticing the pain in my belly was in sync with my back.

That's what I get if I don't slow down, I thought. I knew I'd overdone it that day and promised myself to take it easy the next day.

I downed a Tylenol with a huge glass of water and a quick prayer. That night, a raging storm blew through Seabrook. The power was completely knocked out, plunging the house into darkness. We all went to sleep that night hoping the power would be back on in the morning.

As I tried to fall asleep, thoughts rushed through my mind: *Tomorrow . . . I can't wait for tomorrow. It's been such a long time coming. A lifetime too long.*

Finally, my body's need for sleep conquered my uncomfortable back and belly spasms.

Around two in the morning, I woke up and needed to use the bathroom. I had just returned to bed and settled in when I suddenly heard a pop and felt a whoosh of water soaking my nightclothes and the entire bed. It felt like a flood had rushed out of my body.

I shook Eduard's shoulder. When he woke and looked at me, I said, "I think I ruptured."

Except for two medical school rotations, I hadn't done much training in OB-GYN yet, but I knew what it meant when your water broke at twenty-five weeks. I instantly felt cold with fear. I had to return home. I needed to get to a hospital. Immediately. I already had established OB care at the military base in Ohio where I would complete my residency. Dr. John, my OB-GYN doctor—a future colleague of mine—had shared his cell phone number with me when he heard I would be going out of town for my graduation.

The next couple of hours were a panicked blur: Calling Dr. John who, after learning I planned to drive back to Ohio that early morning to be near home, ordered me to go to the nearest hospital. Waking up Kim, who searched in the dark for a candle so we could see well enough to gather our things and get out to the car. Arriving at the nearby small community hospital, which didn't have the resources to take care of me. Waiting as the OB-GYN on call arrived. Hearing him say the words, "Yeah, cervix is closed. She is grossly ruptured, however." Getting a shot of steroids to speed up fetal lung development, IV antibiotics to prevent infection, and magnesium to avoid labor. Hearing the OB-GYN doctor say, "We cannot keep you here.

Let me make some calls." Waiting more as he called hospital after hospital trying to transfer me: Tufts Medical, Brigham and Women's, Massachusetts General, Dartmouth Medical—but none could take me. They were all full.

The activity around me deepened my terror. Even as a budding doctor, I couldn't reconcile what was happening. I was twenty-five-and-a-half weeks pregnant with my precious baby boy, and he was in danger. This hospital didn't have the equipment or expertise to save him. No one else would take us.

Finally, after more than an hour of waiting, the doctor finally returned. "Brigham and Women's has a space for you," he said.

In exasperation, the good doctor had mentioned to the high-risk OB, a maternal-fetal medicine specialist, on call that night that I was a doctor, and they'd found a bed for me.

Brigham and Women's . . . a sister hospital to Massachusetts General, the place I'd gone with my dermoid cyst all those years back. In the moment, the significance didn't hit me—I was too focused on saving my baby.

They put me in the ambulance, with the sirens on and lights ablaze, and Eduard followed behind us with the car. My baby and I were making an entrance in Boston that very early June 1st morning.

As we drove to the hospital, I attempted to put the pieces of this inexplicable puzzle together. I had enough clinical knowledge to know that even though I hadn't diagnosed this complication before it became an emergency, there were clues I could piece together as to why this happened. Because this was my first pregnancy to make it this far, I had ignored some of my body's signals that something wasn't right, assuming my symptoms were a normal part of pregnancy. I started going over the symptoms I had dismissed: wet underwear, intermittent back pain, uterine tightening, preterm contractions. But those were symptoms, not the underlying condition.

What could be the real cause of this? I didn't have any signs of an infection, no risk factors—and then it hit me.

Could it be the three abortions?

I remembered reading during my OB-GYN rotation that induced vacuum abortion is a risk factor for cervical incompetence, and that the risk increases with the number of abortions due to increasing damage to the cervix. The doctor who examined me said that my cervix was closed. But had it been closed all along, or did it start to lose its strength over time due to the prior forced trauma from my prior abortions?

Even though I wasn't sure I'd ever know the true cause, I could hold the argument for the latter explanation—cervical incompetence—something that later, with my second pregnancy, would prove to be in fact the truth.

For now, I had to remain in the hospital, praying and hoping I wouldn't go into labor or get an infection. I needed to give my baby a chance to grow, to be safe, to survive.

The contrast of this hospital stay couldn't have been starker. When I went in with my dermoid cyst, I was alone, with no one to visit me and no resources to pay for care. Now, I was almost Dr. Luissa Kiprono and being admitted to a hospital that didn't have space a half hour earlier, in part because of who I was and what I represented to the medical community. Instead of a dangerous cyst, I was pregnant with the child I'd dreamed of, and I would be surrounded by loving visitors: my husband, my mom and grandma, my friends. A normal woman with a normal life.

Later that very early morning, I settled into my hospital bed at Brigham and Women's in the penthouse suite. Going from "no beds available" when the doctor had first called to being placed in the penthouse suite was amusing to me and I kept joking about it with Eduard and the hospital staff. The medicine was working: I hadn't gone into labor and the baby was stable. Thank goodness. When Mom and Grandma walked into my room, trailed by Kim and Chad, I instantly started bawling, tears running onto my hospital gown and my chest heaving as my mom wrapped her arms around me in a tight hug. I wasn't sure if my baby was going to be OK, but at least he was safe right now.

As the sun rose over Boston, I realized what I'd miss that day: my graduation ceremony. I knew what my admittance to the hospital meant: I wasn't leaving until my baby was born. My graduation ceremony was that morning, and rather than walking the stage to get my diploma, I would be in a hospital bed, miles in the opposite direction of my college, and worrying over the life of this little human within me—my dear child.

To make things worse, as nurses filtered in and out, they greeted me as "Doctor." Each time, I started to cry. Dr. Kiprono—the thing I'd worked all this time for. The thing I'd anchored to all those years with my father. I would be lying in this hospital bed, hooked up to tubes and monitors, while my classmates filed one by one across the stage.

Why had this happened to my baby and me? And why on the eve of celebrating the thing I'd wanted and worked for my entire life? I had vowed I would not miss this moment for the world. And yet, a higher power, or karma, reminded me that there is at least one exception to any rule. I would be worrying over my baby's life when I should be celebrating one of the most important moments of mine. Since crying and stressing were not doing me or my baby any good, I resolved to embrace the situation.

At seven o'clock that morning, I called the university and explained my situation to the dean of the college. To my shock, he said that, per the rules, I must be present and walk to the podium and physically accept my diploma in order to graduate.

"You don't understand," I said. "I can't walk. I'm in the hospital, pregnant still, with my water broken. I'm not allowed to leave until I have the baby."

"University policy," he said.

So I tried another route: the dean of student affairs. Dean Kelley was our class's favorite member of the faculty. She was a short-statured woman in her late fifties who always dressed professionally, her strawberry red hair neatly combed into a granny bun. Her round blue eyes, rosy cheeks, and caring smile were like a ray of sunshine, inviting us to reciprocate, as if she were saying, "C'mon children, smile! Whatever it is, it can't be that bad." A fierce students' advocate, she was our mother away from home. Students would go to her with good news, requests, grievances, or when in need of a shoulder to cry on, motherly advice, and just about anything else. Through the years of her tenure, she had served as the equivalent of a Catholic priest, hearing many students' confessions, but she didn't need to take an oath to keep our secrets private. She was fair, kind, caring, and loved by students and faculty alike. I went to her office from time to time to chat or just to say hello. I had a great relationship with her and thought she might be able to help.

It being graduation day, she was in her office that early Saturday morning when I called. Without taking a pause to breathe, I explained my dire situation. She listened quietly, then said, "You stay right where you are, child. I will take care of it."

After about an hour, the dean of the college called back: The president of the college was making an exception and agreed to bend policy due to my extenuating circumstance. They would mail my diploma afterward, he said.

"No," I replied. "My husband will drive to the university today and get my diploma."

When I hung up, I looked at Eduard. "You are going to go to my graduation, and you can't come back until you have my diploma."

Amid the fear and overwhelm of the previous few hours, I held on to the one thing I could control. I would have that diploma, proof that I had achieved my dream, a marker of the next stage of my life. The proclamation that I had done it. That I'd beaten the odds to achieve my greatest dream. That I'd overcome the trauma of my past to build a future for myself and my young family. That never again would I be nobody and nothing; instead, I was a doctor.

This was my own life perspective. Everyone has their own unique view of the world, and the value of each prize is determined by the individual. Each one of us must find what personally drives us, no matter how grand or seemingly insignificant, how tangible or distant. That dream becomes a lighthouse in the darkest of nights, enabling one to continue on, to go after that goal no matter what. For me, that lighthouse was becoming a doctor.

No, I couldn't let a day go by without seeing that piece of paper.

Eduard went as requested, accompanied by Chad, who wouldn't let a friend in need go alone. I waited in bed with my dear mom, my grandma, and Kim by my side, trying unsuccessfully to sleep, holding my stomach while shutting my eyes, willing the medicine to keep working. Hours passed. Finally, after what felt like days, Eduard and Chad came into my hospital room. Kim, my mom, and my grandma were still beside my bed, the view of Boston stretching in the panoramic windows behind them.

"Hi, honey," I said. "Do you have it?"

Eduard smiled as he stopped by my bedside and held the thick padded diploma folder out to me. My breath quickened and fingers trembled as I reached to take it, grasping it gently with both hands like it might break. With my knees propped up on the bed, I rested the folder on my thighs and opened it. There it was. The words I'd been waiting for my entire life:

The Board of Trustees of the University of New England, upon
the recommendation of the Faculty of the College of Osteopathic
Medicine, hereby confers upon

Luissa V. Kiprono

the degree of

Doctor of Osteopathic Medicine

together with all the honors, rights, privileges, and responsibilities
thereunto appertaining.

I started to cry, my entire body shaking with deep, complicated sobs: for my baby, for this accomplishment, for my nineteen-year-old self. I closed the folder and set it next to me so my tears wouldn't stain the precious paper.

It was a hard but joyful moment. Bittersweet. It seemed like my life always had to be eventful—I couldn't just have the normal pregnancy or experience walking the graduation stage like everyone else. All I'd wanted, all those years, was to walk across that stage, get my diploma, and walk into my new life as a doctor and mom.

I took a breath, filling my lungs fully and letting out my breath slowly. And then it struck me: *My dream has finally happened. I'm a doctor. I'm going to be a mom. I can finally slow down.* For the first time since I'd left my father's apartment, I didn't feel like I was being chased by my past. I was no longer running after time, trying to gain back what I had lost. The past didn't matter anymore. After all, the past cannot be undone. The present matters most— what we do with today, how we step into tomorrow and the rest of our lives.

I was finally in the present.

I made it. I did it. I achieved my dream. In spite of everything, I achieved my dream.

I reached for the diploma again, rereading its words: Luissa V. Kiprono, Doctor of Osteopathic Medicine.

I am a doctor, I thought. You could take all my possessions but no one could take that away from me. Ever.

America was the place the old me died. But I'd been reborn. And now I was birthing a new life. A precious, unique life. I had a greater purpose than myself now. I was about to become a mom.

I had Eduard hang my diploma on the wall of my hospital room in a beautiful, dark mahogany frame he'd purchased from a frame shop in downtown Boston. After everyone left that night, I lay in the dark of the room, feeling my sweet baby gently roll and squirm safely inside me, the lights of my many monitors dancing on the walls, my diploma lit just enough by the low light of the room to read my name. In that moment, I felt peace. Everything was going to be OK.

Better than OK. It was going to be filled with the simple joys of a normal life.

HE DIED—BUT I LIVED

I wrote this book as a memoir, with birth, death, and rebirth as the theme of my story as an unwilling immigrant to America. What I haven't shared yet is the after—a period of my story that could be its own book. I decided to end the memoir in that hospital room because that's the ending I would have wanted to read during those years with my father. But life is long, and since you're still reading about mine, I'd like to share a bit more of my journey: the resolution with my father, my career and family life, and the mission I'm on today to free more women from their trauma and pain.

First, the resolution. My father died on May 6, 2002, just before my medical school graduation. I was at the dinner table, pregnant with my first son, Jordan, when I got the call from my cousin John—my father's older brother's son—who was living in Cleveland, Ohio.

My father was alone and had been for days before a concerned neighbor came to check on him and found him in the bathtub. Since he was in stage four Parkinson's at that point, his balance was way off, so he must have slipped and fallen while getting in to take a shower.

As I listened quietly to my cousin, not responding, the news registered. My father was dead. Violet, my half-sister, was there, in my old city. Family was gathering to attend the funeral. They were mourning his death.

But I felt nothing. Not sadness. Not pain. Not happiness. Not relief. There was no feeling. Just blankness. Numbness. I wasn't interested in attending his funeral.

And I didn't. The day came and went, and I focused on my growing belly and husband and the house we'd just purchased and my upcoming graduation from medical school.

My sister took care of all of his affairs, and I closed that chapter in my life from a distance. I never shed a tear, never felt sad. I had forgiven him years earlier but not forgotten. And anyway, my father had died long ago in my heart. To be honest, he had never really existed as a father, never lived in a true way in my life as a father should.

He was dead, but I was very much alive, with a life inside me, about to achieve my biggest dream. So I focused on the life ahead of me, not the scarred past behind me.

While writing this book, I did not include my father's death within the main chapters, because his story is not mine anymore. When I left all those years back, when I got the keys to my new place and moved out of his apartment, I broke free of his grip. His story had no power over me anymore. I freed myself and reclaimed agency over my life and my dreams.

Of course, I still sometimes think of Suzette. Her framed picture is part of my office decor to this day.

About a year after I moved out, my father took Suzette out for a car ride. He went into a grocery store and left her in the car with the windows cracked. When he returned, Suzette was gone. He never found her.

My father hadn't wanted Suzette to come with me, but then he had lost her. Or maybe she just couldn't take the solitude anymore and ran away, just like me.

I wonder if after she left, she missed him. I certainly didn't.

When I graduated with my bachelor's degree, I didn't think of my father. When I met and married Eduard, I didn't think of him. When I finished medical school, I didn't think of him. And when I lay in that hospital bed that early morning, fearing for the life of my baby and mourning the missed graduation, I did not think of him. He had ceased to exist to me. His death was simply the final punctuation mark in his nonexistence in my life. And when I changed my name after my divorce, I returned to my true maiden name.

I had forgiven him and made peace within myself, because I knew that carrying anger would only keep me trapped.

But while I forgave and removed him from my life, I didn't forget.

I'll never forget.

I felt, at so many points in my journey, close to being crushed. I retreated within myself for many years, doing everything I could to maintain a sense of stability while living with an unstable person. I found bits and pieces of hope—cracks of life shining through the door to freedom that had been almost shut—and hung on for dear life. Eventually, I overcame. I still overcome.

Yet even after becoming a doctor, my life has not been easy. I did not get lucky breaks, and I've had to work incredibly hard for everything I have accomplished. I learned to become resourceful, flexible, resilient, consistent, proactive, shrewd, and frugal. I learned to discern what I *really* need versus what I want, and to cherish and guard what matters most to me: my health, my close family, and my work. That is it. For me, everything else is replaceable.

Like all trauma and post-traumatic stress disorder (PTSD) victims, I experience anxiety, hypervigilance, insomnia, and digestive issues. Because I had no one to confess to for so many years, I taught myself to internalize and self-process my hardships. Long after becoming a doctor, I worked with therapists specializing in trauma, PTSD, and Eye Movement Desensitization and Reprocessing (EMDR) on three separate occasions, during times when I encountered a great deal of stress from multiple directions.

Stressors continue to come. But now, rather than being alone to fight my demons, I am surrounded by love and support. I recognize stress when it comes and ask for help. This is a core tenet of my ability to thrive today.

And while the book ended in that hospital room, with my diploma on the wall, it was just the beginning of the beautiful life that lay before me, waiting to be experienced.

Today, I am incredibly blessed to be accomplished and healthy. My health is one of my biggest pillars, because without health, it's extremely difficult to accomplish anything.

After medical graduation, I went on to become a board-certified maternal-fetal medicine (MFM) specialist. My designation is rare—there are fewer than 1,300 physicians who specialize in high-risk pregnancy in the entire United States, and roughly 900 who are practicing full time. I've risen to leadership, earning the respect of my peers. In 2018, I founded my own consulting company, World Gateway Perinatal Consultants, and in 2022 its newest addition, the MFM telemedicine division, TeleMedMFM (https://telemedmfm.com), to make my specialty more accessible to pregnant patients throughout rural America and around the globe. While writing this book in 2022, I began working full time in my own company. My goal is to impart medical care to high-risk pregnant women and their unborn babies without barriers. It doesn't matter if you are in rural Texas or sub-Saharan Africa—a woman in need is just a video call away from care. Not only do I get to save lives through my work as an MFM specialist, but I also physically bring my skills to far-flung corners of the globe, like the recent medical mission expedition I completed through the Cordillera Huayhuash, Perú.

My mind and hands now heal others. I save women and babies. I am needed. My work gives me purpose, and I believe deeply that each and every one of us needs a purpose in this world.

As part of my role as a care provider, I also counsel women who don't want to become mothers and support them in their abortion rights. I believe we have a duty to rise up, united, and vote for the freedom to act whichever way we decide when it comes to our bodies. This belief has nothing to do with whether I am pro-life or pro-abortion. It is about the simple, fundamental right to choose my destiny and my future, and have full governance over my body and myself. Taking this basic right away from us women is like removing the right to speak, to pray, to leave, or to stay.

Freedom is the power to have a voice and a choice. To be who you are, to say who you are, to voice your beliefs, and to have the courage to stand and defend them. The right to choose remains the right of every woman, and we must maintain that freedom.

On the personal side, I have my dream family.

My marriage with Eduard eventually ended in divorce, but I remain thankful for the time we shared as well as our two incredible boys, who were born healthy and are thriving today. When our marriage ended, I dusted myself off and focused on rebuilding from the inside out, without a man, without anyone but Luissa. I took time to find myself, with no plans to secure another partner. And after some years alone, when I wasn't looking for love, that's when I met the love of my life: Charles. A man who was already a good person; someone I didn't need to fix and who pushed me to be better. We've built a life of joy and adventure together in San Antonio, Texas.

Charles and my sons are my world.

On top of all this grace, my mom also lives with us. I cherish her presence every single day.

I'm also financially successful. Financial abundance once felt impossible to me. Today, when I make a big purchase, like a trip to Europe or something else I don't "need," I can't help but reflect on my secret sandwiches at D'Angelo's, which took weeks to save up for. Or I think of the envelope of cash from my mom, given with such generous love, that saved my life.

I don't take my financial situation for granted. It took me decades of inner work to move past extreme frugality and be able to enjoy the money I make in my profession. Today, I actually enjoy paying my bills, balancing my checkbook, and reviewing my investments each month—not because I need to be rich, but because money is a security blanket that makes me feel like everything is going to be OK.

On the outside, to someone who doesn't know my story, someone might look at my life in my nice home in San Antonio, with my thriving medical practice and loving husband, and think I've had it easy, that the stars aligned for me. But the truth is that I aligned my own stars. I accepted help when it came: from family and friends who had no idea what was happening but saw I needed help and supported me; from Dr. Levine, my mentor; from my recruiter, SSgt Wallace; from Dean Kelley, who advocated for me and saved graduation; and from my dear friend Kim. I accepted help and stayed connected to my dream, even when my own father tried to rob me of dignity and power.

I am vulnerable, and through this book, I have asserted my vulnerability. For someone who has undergone trauma, this is one of the greatest forms of courage. If you meet me in person, I may look and act tough, but deep inside I am who I have always been, that same girl from Romania who made that journey to America all those years ago: caring, sentimental, trusting, looking for company, hurting, glowing, laughing, crying, loving, and wanting love and compassion back. This book lays it all bare to uncover the real pain behind my story.

Over the year-plus spent writing this book, I asked myself countless times: Would my family and friends, my patients, my colleagues, the world—would they be disappointed to see the real me, the me who went through seven years of hell and fifteen years of incredible resilience to finally reach my goal, to become who I am today?

Or would they—would you—after shedding a tear, celebrate all the good and the blessings, and offer gratitude, so others may have a shoulder to cry on and rest on? So they may also have a way out to freedom?

I first confessed a much-abbreviated version of my story to my friend Kim, some years after moving out of my father's home in 1993. She was the only other person I'd told besides Eduard, and it was incredibly difficult to do. But holding the secret from a close friend was difficult too—it is a heavy burden. And keeping such trauma locked inside only increased my sense of shame.

I am blessed to be here now, sane, having found my purpose, willing and able to share and help guide others on their journeys.

I don't know what led you to pick this book up: Maybe you're in the midst of trauma now or maybe you're out and finding your way. Perhaps you have a mother or sister, a brother or friend who has endured trauma and you want to understand it better so you can support her or him. Maybe you're guiding a patient or client through their journey to healing, and you're hoping to gain insights that can help you do so. Whatever brought you here, I hope you found what you needed in these pages of my life.

Before I close, I want to speak directly to you who are undergoing or healing from trauma. We all carry scars, but trauma goes deeper. It takes a long time to heal. You have to nurture the wounds you carry and be kind to yourself by accepting what has happened to you. And then you must move forward, asking yourself: Now what am I going to do about this? How am I going to create a positive story for my life?

Your future story, like mine, depends largely on how you feel about yourself. You must grieve and process—ideally with the help of a counselor or psychologist—and then find closure so you can move forward. We trauma survivors cannot see ourselves as damaged goods or we will never accomplish anything. Something horrible happened to you; something horrible happened to me. That's a fact that isn't going to change. But if we can't change that fact, what *can* we influence? How can we better ourselves? How can we overcome? How can we take ownership over our future?

I came to realize that it was not God who was going to get me out of the hell I willingly and blindly walked into. It was only me who could do that.

Decide, right now, how you will prevail. How you'll rise above your past experiences to make something of yourself and your life—to bring out the best in you despite what happened.

Your mind is a powerful thing in this regard: It can hold you back or it can help you soar. I chose to soar. I hope you do too.

Traumatic experiences can range widely, and no matter what you've undergone, I want you to know: *I see you.* You are beautiful inside and out. For some reason, life has trampled on you and tried to reduce you to almost nothing. But if you can find that little bit of power within you, you can rise up from the ashes. Yes, you've been a victim. I have too. A victim is someone who has been robbed of their power—and you can't thrive from a position of powerlessness.

There comes a point when you must decide, "I'm done worrying and I'm done being a victim." Instead, you need to ask yourself, "What am I going to do to thrive?"

I know because I've been there. It took me seven years of suffering and many more years of healing to fully find my way. And the truth is, any survivor of trauma is never their "self" again. We uncover a new way to be our old selves. We heal. We grow. We emerge, I hope, better and stronger and with the heart to reach back and hold the hand of another woman just starting her journey.

As you journey through healing, find the thing you want from life and hold your dream close. For me, that dream was to become a doctor. What is it for you? Maybe you want to finish college, start a business, have your own art exhibit, become a dental technician, travel the world, start a podcast, or have a steady job that enables you to gain financial freedom.

Your dream doesn't have to be huge; it simply needs to inspire you. In fact, it doesn't even need to feel like a "dream." If there's nothing you can point to right now that you want to reach for, just hang on to any small rays of hope you can to survive. Nourish these as seeds—always protecting this glimmer of life inside of you, no matter what is happening on the outside— and eventually something will grow from them to become your cornerstone.

I believe everyone has something that can carry them forward with hope, if they look for it.

With a dream or cornerstone firmly anchored in your heart, you then must understand the steps needed to reach it and take action with intentional presence, fortitude, consistency. I credit my ability to accomplish my dream to the daily steps I took to realize it. For many years, that was simply taking a class or two, because that's all I could manage and what my father allowed. But I stuck with it, even when I could only do a little here and there. When I finally gained my freedom and allowed myself to stop for a period of months, I nearly lost momentum. That light of hope for my dream, which had kept me going all those years, nearly went out. My mom—my strength—rekindled it for me so I could light my own fire again. If you have been to hell and back, you must be careful how much slack you give yourself. You must not lose your momentum because it's extremely hard to regain. Once you exit that highway of life, getting back on might feel impossible.

As you drive toward that destination, be patient. Sometimes the car won't go as fast as you'd like. Sometimes it breaks down on the side of the road and you need to fix it before you can move on. Maybe you lose your job or experience a medical issue or lose someone. Life is not within our control, but we must deal with the challenges as they come and keep going. Keep your eyes, and heart, on the beautiful possibility ahead—a life without trauma. A life of healing. A life of experiencing the range of human feelings beyond pain: love, joy, peace, contentment, hope.

As you progress toward your dreams, find someone to anchor you. For me, that was my mom and our conversations every Sunday. It was also Suzette, my cat who loved me unconditionally during my hardest times. Who is that person or animal, or even sacrosanct memory, for you? Choose carefully. Select someone or something who will be a source of steadiness in the storm. Even if you choose not to disclose your trauma, which I did for many years, lean on them anyway. Let their strength become yours.

And finally, find moments of joy along the way, even in the hardest times. Do something that reaches into your soul. For me, walking in the graveyard with Suzette was the respite I needed to be able to recharge and survive another day. Running became a place to reenergize and meditate. What is your respite? What recharges you? Maybe it's a blessed place, whether in the forest or under a tree near your house, where you can sit and just be. Maybe it's journaling. Maybe it's praying. You will find your sacred outlet, you just to have to believe in it and it will reveal itself. Then stick with it. I believe that everyone can find sacred time every day, even if it's just five minutes.

As you align your own stars, I hope my story will help you see the possibility within yourself. Tell yourself, "I can do this." By finding even the faintest light of hope, you can begin to uncover the power within you to overcome. It doesn't matter how long it takes you to achieve your dreams, just that you get there eventually. Once you arrive, that glory is all yours. The only person you need to prove anything to is yourself.

As you pursue your dreams, you will sometimes fall short. You may even trip and fall flat on your face in front of a metaphorical theatre of critics. But get back up. Connect to your power. Find the strength to pick up the pieces and keep going.

Don't give up.

No matter what.

Against all odds.

Keep going.

Until the day you become your complete self.

Again.

AUTHOR'S NOTE

Writing this book . . . what a gargantuan process it has been. Wow. To be perfectly honest, I began this book about a year after I landed on American soil. I wrote the first chapter in Romanian and then tucked it away for close to thirty years. Then, one morning—about five years ago—I found I was recording my thoughts once more, and on a somewhat regular basis. But I soon came to the glaring realization that at the rate I was going, while tackling the daily routine of life and work, I would likely finish my creation, this book, in another twenty years, if at all.

After a lot of research on the internet, and after an emotional and heart-wrenching conversation with her, I started my creative journey with Stacy Ennis, who became my book coach. Stacy, you have my gratitude and admiration for the kindness and fortitude to literally walk along with me in Algarve, Portugal, and virtually walk along with me here in the States, through this journey of deep vulnerability. Thank you for helping me find the strength to bring my book out into the world.

Many thanks to my beta readers for their enthusiasm and constructive feedback. You fined-tuned my manuscript in a very meaningful and touching way.

Heartfelt thanks to the StacyEnnis.com team for editing and proofing the manuscript and to the Greenleaf Book Group team for meeting with me in person and via multiple Zoom meetings. Your knowledge, insight, and coaching in production, publishing, and marketing guided me in understanding a process that I had zero knowledge about.

Thank you, Jim Van Hook, from the bottom of my heart for enthusiastically accepting my ask to write the thoughtful foreword. Your professional and personal experience homed in on important aspects of my book.

My deepest gratitude to all the humans, too many to name here, who have helped me through these years, whether knowingly or unknowingly, and without whom I would have never been able to write my story as it stands right now: triumph over trauma, light out of darkness, strength through vulnerability.

To my mother, Aurora, for her steadfast and unshaking way of believing in me. To Kim, my dearest and best friend ever—for non-judgmentally listening and being there for me through all these years.

Last but not least—Mr. Bold: You bring out the better in me. Thank you for being the wind that helps me soar higher.

Dr. Luissa K.

ABOUT THE AUTHOR

Let's get started. Who am I? Dr. Luissa K, a women's doctor and healer of souls.

The desire to help people inspired and fueled me from a young age. Becoming a women's physician—first an obstetrician-gynecologist, and then a maternal-fetal medicine specialist—has allowed me to fulfill this desire over the past twenty years.

When I cared for patients of all ages and from all walks of life—through my residency and fellowship, in academia, as a military doctor, and later in private practice—I discovered a privilege incomparable with anything I had ever experienced: the power of doing good, making a difference in people's lives, and helping them regain something that most of us mistakenly take as status quo, our health.

Thirty-six years ago, one month shy of turning nineteen years old—a refugee from former communist Romania—you could say that I was born again. I gained resilience, experienced the rollercoasters of a new journey, mastered a new language, a new system, and a new way of life.

One thing remained steadfast through it all: my desire to help people heal. And I started to realize that people need emotional and spiritual healing as well as the physical, organic form. This realization led me to my next chapter, writing my first non-fiction book based on the first fifteen years of my reborn life. Having the tenacity to take this step meant coming full circle spiritually, making it my mission through my own vulnerability and life experience to help my fellow women and patients face their own fears, overcome perceived shortcomings, and pursue their inner value.

In the summer of 2022, when my employer's practice closed its doors in San Antonio, I knew I had the opportunity of a lifetime. I could serve my two life missions: professionally, through my maternal-fetal telemedicine practice *TeleMed MFM*, I could make high-risk pregnancy care available to all women beyond borders or geographical limitations; and holistically, through my book *PUSH, THEN BREATHE: Trauma, Triumph, and the Making of an American Doctor* and my platform, *Dr. Luissa K*, I could reach out to all women to join the quest for self-empowerment.

I invite you to join in this search for self-empowerment, defining intentional presence, and resilience.

Dr. Luissa Kiprono, MBS, MBA

Notes

Notes